The Rogers' Fa.

May you always

. . . hold a gentle thought

the Nay's

Soft Prose, Poetry & Short Stories

Gene Nay

Gene Nay

authorHOUSE®

true love

Of all the treasures
in all God's worlds
and all His skies above,

life's greatest gift,
most precious gem,
is that we call true love.

I've searched the world
and I can see,
the answer now is clear to me,

the price at which
true love is bought
is just to . . .
. . . *hold a gentle thought*

Gene Nay

AuthorHouse™
1663 Liberty Drive
Bloomington, IN 47403
www.authorhouse.com
Phone: 1-800-839-8640

. . . hold
a gentle
thought

First printing of 2nd edition

Published by AuthorHouse 05/30/2013

ISBN: 978-1-4817-0356-7 (sc)
ISBN: 978-1-4817-0355-0 (hc)
ISBN: 978-1-4817-0358-1 (e)

Library of Congress Control Number: 2013900239

Dedication

I dedicate this book to the countless people who provided immeasurable influence, encouragement and suggestions in putting it together. To a special few who, even more than I, made this publication happen.

I thank you Sue for challenging me to put into words a simple explanation. A task that made me realize I could do more with words than I had ever dreamed.

To Celeste, Sunny, Shaun, Alex, Paula & all the critters, Mary, Jim, Stephen, Scott, Elaine, Don & Janice, Alan & Noleen, Roberto, Chet & Carol, Frank & Monica.

To Popo, James & Rita, Jay & Lily, John & Grace, and, Shana & Tom who's "mother hen" approach walked me through all that had to do with the process.

To all the Klemmer folks and the many others that are in my thoughts and prayers always.

To the printers and publishers for all their help.

To the person who jump-started this book, Karin Jaros of the Morton Arboretum in Lisle, Illinois, who currently holds the record as the busiest person I know and yet somehow manages to get it done.

To Margo, the purest human being I have ever known and to David, Christy, Vickie, and with great respect to Bill.

I owe a very special thank you to Lady, without whom none of these words would have ever arrived in the hands and hearts that are now holding this book.

I thank all of you.

Gene Nay

the day is warm
and comfortable,
warm from the sun
and comfortable
from thoughts of you.

Contents

Section I Soft Prose . . .

Section 2 Poetry . . .

Section 3 Stories, Talks & Experiences

Section 4 Guest Poets . . .

Loneliness is
the greatest hell,
for where is the joy
of giving?

About the Author

Here's a brief background of Gene Nay for your review. Going straight from High School into the United States Air Force he completed Ground Radar Maintenance Technician training and was selected to become a Technical Instructor. Completing Instructor Training he was transferred to Airborne Bombing, Navigation, and Computer Systems on what was then the highly classified Q-24 Radar System. When discharged from the Air Force he went to work for North American Aviation at the Rocketdyne test facility and later for Burroughs Electro Data, a company developing high speed computers. His sideline interest in sales brought him greater rewards as a productive salesman. He did well and won a position as Vice President and General Manager of a manufacturer's representative company on behalf of a dozen companies selling missile parts to missile manufacturers in the western United States. When the cold war ended so did the missile business. He was hired to work at Newport News Ship Building and Dry Docks installing radar systems on nuclear submarines and the John F. Kennedy the first nuclear aircraft carrier. He continued to develop his sales skills which brought him to the attention of people at National Housewares. He worked there for many years and was a quality producer, trainer and distributer and won his Master of Sales Award. With the divestiture of ATT, he became an independent long distance telephone service provider and remained in that field until he retired.

About the Book

Many years ago suffering a series of deep personal losses, Gene wanted to die and planned to. Yet he knew that was wrong. Writing about these feelings eased the pain. Desperate to be able to hold some *gentle thoughts*, he began writing in earnest, reinterpreting these happenings for himself. Soon he could see other points of view which enabled him to cope. Focusing on setting these experiences to rhythm and rhyme took his attention from the pain. As his interest and capabilities grew so did his collection of writings. Sharing these words seemed to help others too. People had constantly encouraged him to publish. He began giving book signings, readings and public speaking. They would also return bringing others to hear these words. He wondered if he could put into prose, poetry and/or short stories the issues that he found difficult to deal with. If an incident was too sensitive, painful or joyous to think about, could he make it easier to cope with? Through the exercise of putting these experiences into one or more of these three choices of expression he became able to deal with his most extraordinary difficulties. Whether positive or negative, he could cope! Some readers say that their applying these principles gets good results. Now he just wants to put these words into the ears, hands and hearts of those who also seek to be able to . . .

. . . hold a gentle thought.

*May we always
be able to experience
someone's unsolicited
smile.*

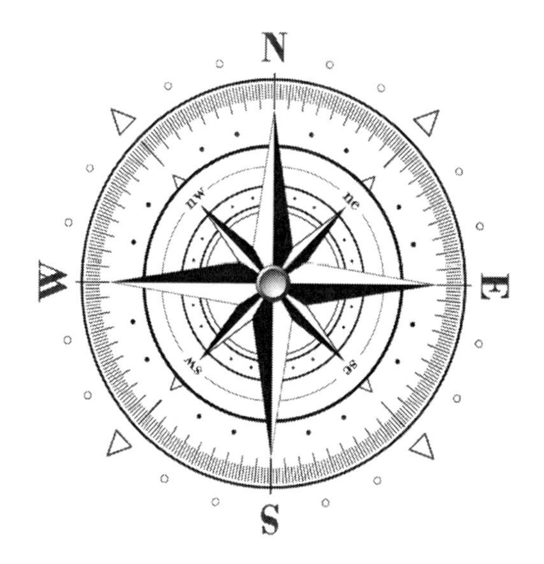

Section 1 Soft Prose . . .

I seek from life . . .

days filled with natures bounteous blessings
and the enjoyment of labors accomplished.

nights of burdens released, rest acquired,
the sharing of companionship and peace.

music granting mental images
of moments too precious to forget.

friends who value and accept me as I am,
to whom I may lend my gentle thoughts.

my love upon whom I may bestow
the material, spiritual and physical
rewards of adoration that
we may cherish and be cherished
by each other.

kisses of kindness, tenderness,
passion and compassion
in abundance and profusion.

marriage that inspires us
by the treatment we render
to keep each other first in our hearts
so there will be room for none other.

the holy act of intimate love that gives
and takes fulfillment from fulfilling.

an understanding
of the agony
and the joy
we bring to ourselves
by our own choices.

death that is the opening of a new portal
where bonding takes on a higher meaning
than terrestrially promised,

Heaven, where God's good purposes for us
are fully revealed and experienced forever.

Gene Nay

I seek from the day . . .

sunrise, cool, quiet,
life's pre-awakening time.

the beginning sounds
of animal, bird, insect
and man.

the growing rustle
as life forms hustle
to acquire their needs.

takings, leavings,
laughings, grievings.

a time to wish and accomplish.

to be involved enough
to forget my personal stress.

most of all
a sense of harmony
and balance.

Gene Nay

I seek from the night . . .

a sanctuary from the day
where I can release my burdens.

a peaceful retreat
where my soul can feed
        on the good things
                I discovered through the day.

a hint of jasmine
to remind me of
        the moments I wish to recall.

the flame of a candle
somewhere to signify
        that I am not forgotten.

someone I revere within reach
that I may touch to assure
        that even in my slumber
                I am aware of them.

a gentle time for the fulfillment
of our needs
and for expressions
of our adoration.

the time when we must accept
the fact that our own
unconscious helplessness
requires that we
resign ourselves
into the hands of He
that watches over
us all.

Gene Nay

I seek from music . . .

a passageway of sound
through which I may escape
my oppressions and tribulations.

the opportunity to close my eyes
and see the warm and gentle moments
I wish to recall.

a picture painted
in composition and lyrics.

mental excursions,
good, bad, happy, sad.
A period of evaluation
and letting go.

an awakening
of solitary companionship
filled with reverie and memory.

sonic food for my soul.

Gene Nay

I seek from a friend . . . .

a gentle smile
to lessen my times of turmoil.

the opportunity
to show kindness.

a laugh,
a tear,
a sympathetic ear.

the wisdom
not to let me ask
more of them
than their loyalty
will allow them to give.
a helping hand.

the courage to criticize
my foolishness
and enough caring
to enjoy my triumphs.

a measure of diplomacy
    to overcome
        my times of irritability.

a talk at sunset
    when the soul
        is influenced
            by natures quiet moment.

I seek nothing more
    from a friend
        than I am willing to give,
            that I may be equal
                to the value
                    of that friendship.

Gene Nay

I seek from my Lady . . .

an intimate intellectual relationship.

one in which
    the inner truths of our beings can unite
        and fully appreciate each other.

the joys of learning to know
    and accept our differences
        and to have more because of them.

to be able to communicate
    on any subject, at any depth,
        for any length of time
            without misgivings or shame.

to be able to be
    natural and yet be concerned.

to be able to be intimate
    without being physical.

to be able to be loved
without making love.

to make love
without demanding love.

to be above all
honest, gentle, understanding,
appreciative and compassionate
with each other.

to taste of each others cup,
leaving us both
richer for the tasting
and thus fulfilling
our mutual needs.

Gene Nay

I seek from a kiss . . .

the sensation of becoming
totally unaware of myself.

the involuntary tuning
of all my faculties
to listen for response.

to be unhurried,
so not to miss
the joy of anticipation.

letting go of all other realities
through the slow realization
of spreading rapture.

softly touching, tenderness,
blending, gentle pressures.

swirling senses,
lowering fences.

the growing
    of suppressed desire.

falling together,
    unaware of the fall.

concluding that
    nothing else exists.

the ultimate sensitivity.

Gene Nay

I seek from marriage . . .

a sharing of life's simple complexities
and its complex simplicities.

a return of the effort expended
to make our relationship endure.

to give and receive total assurance,
that through our certainty,
we may act and be acted upon naturally.

to serve, cheer, console and revere,
and be helper, lover,
companion and friend.

to endeavor to keep each other
first in our hearts,
so there will be room
for none other.

to call each day
upon the divine source
to nourish
and strengthen our bond.

to grant forgiveness,
love and fulfillment readily
and joyfully forever.

Gene Nay

I seek from intimacy . . .

the supreme moment of sharing.

the physical act
of minds touching.
the unification
of souls and emotions.

the gradual spiraling climb,
urged on by necessity
to achieve the apex
from where two
can momentarily look down
into the sea of tranquility
before abandoning
themselves to the miracle
of plunging inevitably into
the rapture of mutual joy.

the ultimate empathy
where fulfillment
is the reward of fulfilling
as two become one.

Gene Nay

I seek from my family . . .

a gentle morning, "Good morning,"

the assurance that if the opportunity
to be of assistance is noticed,
help will arrive
without being summoned.

a sincere attitude of gratitude
by recognizing the spiritual value
of providing service to each other.

their agreed understanding that
courtesy, pleasantness, patience,
meekness, humility, respect,
loyalty, love and genuine concern
are the attitudes they will encounter
in the celestial kingdom
and that the Lord
has provided them a family
on which to practice
and develop these attributes.

verification that they realize
that they have the power
to make all of our lives together
a beautiful experience,
but only if they know
how important it is
for them to get out of themselves
before they loose the opportunity
to love and be loved by each other.

their conclusion
that the only things
they can take with them
when they leave this life behind
is their relationships,
especially that of their family
and their creator
who loved them enough
to give them a still small voice
to guide them
in the choices they make
so He can take them safely home.

Gene Nay

I seek to understand . . .

my gratitude at recognizing
  the value of regret.

my sorrow
  for those whom
    I've made weep.

my joy that I can
  weep for others.

my pain that I don't
  weep often enough.

my delight when I
  care to much for others.

my shame when I
  care too much for myself.

my joy that
I can cry happy tears.

my puffing up
to make myself appear
more than I am.

my gladness
when I consider
all that I have accomplished.

my regret when
I must admit to myself
what I could have done.

my agony from mistakes
that I will remember
until I become pure enough
to let those memories go.

Gene Nay

I seek from death . . . .

a parting from temporal matters.
a new beginning.
the opening of a new portal.

the putting aside of the menial
and focusing fully on the spiritual.

a genuine completion
of the tasks before me
so I may set about
the next step in His plan.

the opportunity
for additional growth,
a major step in maturing.

the guidance to let go of guilt
for things unaccomplished,
in order to attain
the accomplishments needed
to proceed to the next level
of development.

a place where the bonds
of human relationships
take on a deeper perspective.

a natural migration
to a realm
where I may glorify my love,
myself and my creator
for His good purposes.

Gene Nay

I seek from Heaven . . .

In a poem I call Charlie and
the Reverend, I pictured an 11
year old Charlie having a talk
with his minister, the Reverend
Halared. That old, old saying
about "out of the mouths of babes . . ."
struck me. Charlie speaks of
a Heaven that I can understand
and that I long for us all to find.
This talk and experience is found in
Section 3 and took place at a community
"Easter Sunrise Service" where I was one
of a dozen or so speakers representing local
Christian Denominations, I call it **about prejudice.** Because I am particularly pleased
with Charlie's message I have chosen to refer
you there until I can come up with what I feel is
a better explanation of Heaven.

Gene Nay

When I really
have something to say,
let me say it
in a pleasing way

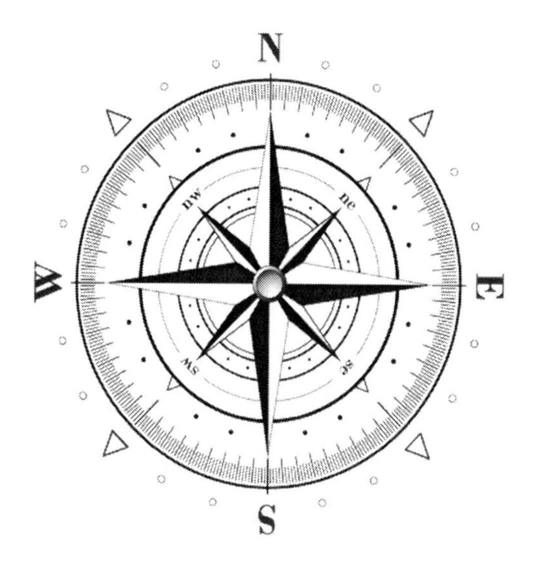

Section 2 Poetry . . .

alone

Is there a way
  to pass the day
    while your away?

It seems so wrong
  without your song,
    it's much too long.

I hope to see
  that it can be
    that you miss me

as I miss you
  and wish we two
    could say and do

the things that please
  and put at ease
    and give the keys

from Him above,
  the blessings of
    our lasting love.

Gene Nay

beautiful scars

The beauty of my scars
is the vulnerability
I experienced
in obtaining them.

Not treasuring
the hurt,
but how
I became hurtable.

Gene Nay

before

Take a look at sunshine,
take a look at rain. Take a look at happiness
and take a taste of pain.

It seems you must know one
to understand the other. Got'ta know your enemy
to recognize a brother.

Life can't be a simple thing.
It wasn't meant to be. Realizing that you're blind
to ever hope to see.

The plans that we are surest of
often go astray. The one you want to turn to you
may simply turn away.

If I were granted just one thing,
I'd like to know that I, could see an opportunity
before it passed me by.

Gene Nay

May you find
the kind of life
that comes to those
who seek to live
a kind life

black and white

Some may say ’tisn’t right
to walk the line ’tween black and white.

The easiest judg’in done today
is done by fools with naught to pay.

It’s always easy to say what’s wrong
with roads you’ve never walked along.

If you want to understand
and have the courage to walk the land,
and let the bigots spit where you stand
and still not loose each others hand,

then in your heart for you ’tis right
to walk the line ’tween black and white.

Gene Nay

changed

Endings somehow seem to start
new beatings in an empty heart.
Is it safe again to try ?
Can we once more learn to fly?

Mercy comes in different ways,
darkest nights, then brightest days.
Storms, lightening, joy and sadness,
thunder, flood, healing gladness.

Satan tried to make us quit,
filled our heads with thoughts of it.
Should we split and run or stay?
Endless troubles in our way.

Count them all and do the math,
the difficulties in our path.
Now's the time, we have to choose,
will we win or must we loose?

We agreed to Fathers plan,
swore they'd never say we ran.
We told Father, "We can do it!"
We assured Him we'd stick to it.

We threw down our walls of pain,
together to start anew again.
Make a place beneath the sun
filled with flowers, love, and fun.

Quench me with a sip of life,
help me put aside my strife.
I'll be your cup, you be mine,
we can share life's sweetest wine.

May our joy be found in givin'
gentle thoughts, and peaceful livin'.
I will grant your great request.
You will know we're truly blest.

We can share with any friend,
from beginning to the end.
We've recovered, *changed* our fate,
prayers are answered, life's so great!

Gene Nay

Charlie and the Reverend

Charlie was a curious boy
and hungered so to learn.
Heaven, he'd heard, is full of joy
and hell a place to burn.

He had so many questions on
the things that preachers say.
Today we live, tomorrow we're gone.
Will we collect or pay?

He had to know what lay ahead,
and so he so he sought the truth
and cornered Reverend Halared
behind the preachers booth.

Please dear Reverend tell me now,
though I'm just eleven,
what's it like, if some how
I should go to Heaven?

Said the Reverend, "Now don't you worry,
you're just a youth, you see."
Poor Charlie's hands waived in a flurry,
"But I've asked you seriously."

The Reverend saw the boy had meant it
when he had made his plea.
Sensing Charlie might resent it
he said, "Now let me see.

You want to know what Heaven's about,
and that's alright with me.
You needn't fret or ever doubt
it's quite the place to be.

Heaven's a wondrous and joyful place
With streets of gold and jewels.
Where God can live and show His face
and never deal with fools.

It's filled with music forever more,
  sweet songs of praise for our King,
    with nothing to want or hunger for
      forever well sing and sing."

The Reverend had told what he believed
  and told it straight and truly,
    but Charlie seemed so unrelieved
      as though he'd been treated cruelly.

"How could the child be so disappointed?"
  The Reverend wanted to know.
    To gaze forever upon the Anointed
      would please the Reverend so.

The Reverend couldn't comprehend it
  and said, "Please Charlie, sit down.
    Heaven is God's, I didn't invent it.
      Why does it make you frown?"

Charlie sat down and sadly said,
"How could I have been so wrong?
I've always felt that when we are dead
there'd be more to Heaven than song.

I pictured a home, a place of my own
with endless things to do,
where I could let the God I've known
teach me just like you.

I thought of myself all big and grown up,
learning what God likes to do.
Visions of trees and flowers sown up
in ways that He only knew.

I dreamed of suns and planets and stars
like those I see in the sky,
of shaping and placing the nears and the fars
under Fathers watchful eye.

It hurts me to think that He'd spend His days
and want nothing more to do
than listen to praise and songs and hoorays
from all, and from me, and from you.

I thought He would share and teach us to care
and tell us of secrets He knows.
It seemed He'd want more than for us to stare
at His face, and His throne, and His clothes.

I'm so sorry sir, but the Heaven you know
is not what I had hoped for.
I must admit that I thought He'd show
how to do things and much more.

I see I was wrong and I hope He'll forgive.
My folly is that of my age.
Now that it's clear, as long as I live,
I'll sing to Him page after page.

When I get there I'll know all the songs,
especially those He likes best.
I'm sure I'll feel I'm where I belong
and that I'm so truly blessed.

Thank you Reverend for all your advice.
You've been so helpful to me.
I'll study real hard and sing so nice.
I'll make Him so proud, you'll see."

"Charlie's a man now," said Reverend Halared
as the boy slowly walked away.
"He's let go the dreams that filled his head.
Reality will now bear sway.

Why it sounded like the boy had believed
he'd become like God above."
The grateful Reverend was so relieved.
He had straightened him out with love.

Still something in what the child had said,
had made the Reverend recall,
words of the Savior spoke in his head.
could he remember it all?

In Romans 8 it seems like I read,
"We're children of God and His heirs."
Revelations 21, there it said.
"He that overcomes all is theirs."

The Reverends hand was searching to find
the switch to turn out the light.
"Have I just snuffed the light in his mind?
Could it be the boy had been right?"

Gene Nay

come live with me

Come live with me and be my own
before this chance for us has flown,
lest it be lost down lonely years
filled with hollow, empty fears.

Come live with me while there is still
the time to all our dreams fulfill,
lest those dreams should all be lost
and thus alone we pay the cost.

Come live with me that we may know
the joy of watching flowers grow,
lest all the blooms should wither and die
from opportunities gone by.

Come live with me that we may find
a gentle peace to ease our mind,
lest we should loose the tender touch
as we have often feared so much.

Come live with me and take my hand,
you know as well as I it's planned,
lest we should fret and wonder how
our lives could grow to be by now.

Come live with me and fill the void,
  fulfill the love we've so enjoyed,
    lest we be cursed as idol fools,
      forsaking all our gems and jewels.

Come live with me my lady fair
  and bring your treasure, small and rare,
    lest we should reach to late to hold,
      before the petals all unfold.

Come live with me for you can see
  the way our lives were meant to be,
    lest we be left with dreams untried
      for what if one of us had died.

Come live with me and bring the joy
  of Eden, Shangri-la, and Troy,
    lest we let go the chance to give
      your smallest bloom the right to live.

Come live with me and do it now
  for we have learned the why and how.
    Lest we forever empty be,
      I ask you please come live with me.

Gene Nay

Too much, too soon,
too little appreciated

comfort

Every night and all of my days
you seem to be with me in so many ways.

You're the special spot in the back of my mind,
where I can seek refuge from troubles I find.

You're there in a song, some haunting refrain.
I listen along and see you again.

You're people, or places, you're mystical faces.
You're constantly with me in endless traces.

Reminders of you can always be found.
All I need do is just look around.

At times life's cold and hardly worth while,
I think of your face and warm to your smile.

You're always with me in the comfort you give
and so I must love you as long as I live.

Gene Nay

communication

Communication
    seems to be
a very difficult way,

an incantation
    lies in me
that is a way to say,

things that seem
    to mean so much
tell what I have in mind.

As in a dream
    so hard to touch
and oh, so hard to find.

More than all
        that I can speak
I wish for you to know,

the large and small
        of what I speak,
the truth, I love you so.

Gene Nay

Growing up
is the process
of realizing
it may never happen

constant shade of blue

Ever wonder where you're goin'?
Seems I always do.
Draggin' days n' nights are showin'
a constant shade of blue.

Travlin' down the same old road,
seein' where I've been.
Livin's such a heavy load.
Same old world of sin.

Got'ta be some way to change
the way I pass the time.
Gladly trade the color blue
for a simple shade of lime.

So many things to think about
but little left to do.
I could really do without
this constant shade of blue.

Gene Nay

decreed

I've sent you this flower
to brighten your day.
I've filled it with love
cause now it's okay.

There are some things
we need to make clear,
things that I really
am hoping to hear.

I don't mean to press you
or cause you concern.
'Tis simply your feelings
I'm eager to learn.

Since being allowed
a glimpse of your heart,
I'm given no peace
since we've been apart.

I hope that no other
has lead you away,
cause I've waited long
for this very day.

If you've chosen another
I will understand,
though all I desire
seems so close at hand.

Is there a chance
that you'd like to talk?
Perhaps have a bite
or just take a walk.

I tremble with fear
for what you might say.
I'm frightened, I'm scared
but can't run away.

Perhaps we will find
what both of us need,
and that it's from Heaven
that this was decreed.

Gene Nay

encounters

Chance encounters,
    ever rare,
        reassure
    that someone's there.

What's the signal,
    how to sign,
        'touching someone
    else's mind?

Dare I speak
    of what I feel,
        thus my hopefulness
    reveal?

Words to say
    elusive thoughts,
        vague and
    inconclusive thoughts.

Where's the way
to let it show,
how am I
to let you know?

Will I appear
a child in school,
thought by you
to be a fool?

If you have
these feelings now,
will I know
and if so . . . . how?

Gene Nay

finders

It seems to me
that there must be
a way that life should go.
A master plan
to guide each man
in things they do not know.

Can there be some
help that will come
from hints along the way?
I think we find
a certain kind
of help throughout the day.

If we but will
hear all the still
small voices from inside,
we're sure to see
our destiny
can't long within us hide.

All you must do
is listen to
the quiet reminders.
Give it a try
as life goes by
seekers are the finders.

Gene Nay

When a man grows old enough to
truly appreciate a woman's favors
he doesn't get them anymore, ...
or is it the other way around?

hello

This is just a small, “Hello”,
from a lonely guy.
You can simply tell me, “Go”,
and I will say, “Goodbye”.

If you think some friendly talk
would help you pass the time,
please don’t make me take “the walk”.
cause you may find that I’m,

feelin’ just about the same
and it’s even likely,
that if you let me tell my name
you may even like me.

Is it possible that you
would like some “company”?
You may find that it is true
that you’ve a friend in me.

Gene Nay

hon

Why'm I walkin' on the cielin'?
Cuz I've got the dangdest feelin'.

Why'm I in this strange cun'dition?
I just gotsum am-unition!

What's the am-unition I've found?
M'baby'll be comin' round!

Why's it so import'nt t'me?
She's th'one I most want t'see!

Why is she sucha special one?
Cuz she's m'everluvin' hon!

Gene Nay

I'll be here

I'll be here
in your need.

I'll heal your wounds
when the time comes.

I'll be your safe harbor
in the midst of tempests.

I'll grant you sanctuary,
a warm nest for your troubled soul.

I'll bring you sunshine, rainy days,
flowered breezes, and gentle ways.

I'll be here
when you come home.

Gene Nay

I'm not the man

I'm not the man I could have been
    and I may never be,
because I've witnessed so much sin
    and it's affected me.

I will tell you of these sins,
    some I still can see.
I fear that they've forever changed
    the me I'd hoped to be.

I saw a man that said
    "Follow my example."
He took advantage of his friends
    and that was just a sample.

Then there's the man who lives
    as though he's clean and pure.
he takes back all he gives
    plus double to be sure.

I've seen a man who broke his word
    and turned his face away.
He rejected all he heard
    no matter what they'd say.

I've seen an awful pride
    keep one from doing right.
Not man enough to look inside
    he kept it up for spite.

One brought pain and heartbreak
    caused by negligence,
and then he tried to cover up
    by pleading innocence.

You may say it's not enough
    these reasons that I give.
You say it's up to me to choose
    the way I want to live.

There are more sins I have seen
    worse than all before.
Some of them have been so bad,
    let me tell you more.

I have even seen a man
    so woe-be-gone and lazy,
were someone to depend on him
    he nearly drove them crazy.

There's a man that played with minds
    and led them far astray.
He convinced them they could wrong
    and never have to pay.

And then a man who's wife
    was good and pure and chaste.
He chose to live a sinful life
    and made it all a waste.

I've seen a servant of the Lord
    raise his arm in hate,
then tell others "Drop the sword
    and find the Pearly Gate".

A man I know shunned his God
    to go another way,
in spite of all his friends and family
    tried in vain to say.

I've seen so many ugly things
    it really is a shame.
This is why I have to tell you
    where to lay the blame.

If you wonder why I blame
    all the sins I've shown,
I'm not the man I could have been
    these sins are all my own.

Gene Nay

it took so long

It took so long,
down so many roads.
Wanderin' lonely,
draggin' life's loads.

Many a season
and lots of years.
Huntin' a reason
for all of our tears.

You travelin' your way,
me goin' mine,
needin' direction
and seekin' a sign.

All of the sorrow
and pain we've been through.
A dream we could borrow,
a heart that was true.

Who would've thought
from worlds so apart,
that we'd find each other
and new dreams would start.

We'd never have guessed,
I'm sure it's true,
that we could be blessed
with one dream for two.

Now it's begun,
we're each others song
and somehow I'm glad
that it took so long.

Gene Nay

joy

I give to you sharing
to prove my love is caring.

I give compassion
to keep our love in fashion.

I give affection
to give our love protection.

I give tenderness
to help relieve the stress.

I give all this to you
while hoping you'll give too.

Give these things to me
and then I'm sure you'll see

the joys that will be ours
can take us to the stars.

Gene Nay

just another night alone

Someone is aware of you,
now you notice it.
The eyes are brown instead of blue,
somehow it doesn't fit.
Is it just your ego,
because you want it so?

Why is there this strange appeal?
What is it makes you look?
Do you want so much to feel?
Are you an open book?
Is this the thing you need?
Is it a planted seed?

What could ever come of this?
Surely not a thing.
Can't help wonder if a kiss
would start the bells to ring.
Why's there someone else there?
Sure do like the hair.

Now they are about to leave.
S'pose it's just as well.
Do you just want to believe?
One can never tell.
Now we'll never know
if it would ever grow.

Still it tingles in your mind,
seems like something's there.
Wonder if you'd ever find
if you could really care?
Shut it out, silly self!
Put your daydreams on the shelf!

It's just another night alone
like all the rest to me.
Familiar feelings that I've known
won't get the best of me.
Don't let yourself think twice,
but it might have been so nice.

Gene Nay

Lady

The Lady came along
so gentle as she smiled.
Her movement was her song,
a lovely sort of child.
A mystic image in my mind,
unreconciled.

Dreams and fantasies sublime
swirled a haze of blue.
Never thought that given time
the wistful dream was true.
Realities pervade the mind,
yet undefiled.

Fragile thoughts, like grains of sand
filled the void design,
slipping softly through the hand,
sad the hand was mine.
The chains of freedom held her mind,
unreconciled.

Feast on unreality,
as I gaze upon
ghosts within a memory,
never to be gone.
A flower lives within our mind,
yet undefiled.

Gene Nay

Are there moments
when you stop
to wonder if
I think of you?

"life's begun"

I thought my life had all but past,
    it seemed the good just couldn't last
I thought it's over, then suddenly,
    smiling eyes were smiling at me.

I've stumbled on a brand new life,
    and captured such a lovely wife.
She's become my morning sun
    and filled my days with "life's begun."

How long it seemed there's no one there,
    'till I'd forgotten how to care.
Then she was there and it was fun,
    my world was changed by "life's begun."

I must admit that now it's true
    that love has changed my point of view.
God grant she'll always be the one
    for it's through her that "life's begun."

Gene Nay

love lost

Gentle thoughts and peaceful places
help me wipe away the traces
of the dream that could have been
were it not for doubts within.

Once again I see her face,
simple beauty, smiling grace.
Open arms that took me in,
made my gentle thoughts begin.

Sunny days of summer fun.
Evenings with my precious one.
Tears and laughter in our joy,
we could scale the walls of Troy.

You can guess what must be told.
It was more than we could hold.
Now she's gone my lady fair,
sparkling eyes and silken hair.

So I search through tears of sorrow
in the hope that I may borrow
just a gentle thought or two.
Who will lend them, maybe you?

Gene Nay

may I

May I approach you
simply for nearness
and not make you feel
pressured?

May I touch you softly,
giving calm,
lending comfort,
for I need to be close?

May I hold your attention
for a little while,
tasting your presence,
ever learning your mind?

May I feel your lips touch mine,
dissolving old dreams,
finding fresh fantasies,
blending splendidly?

May I enfold you
in the circle
of my arms
and release you?

May I look at you,
gently, quietly,
soaking up
your soul?

May I cling to you,
desperately
needing you
yet restrained?

May I have you
only in that magic
and wondrous moment
when you want me?

Gene Nay

my waiting heart

Hurry to me!
I revel
in the thought of you.
I dare not ponder goodbye
for it would steal
my present joy.

Oh, that the torment of hope
could be fulfilled!
If only your time
and mine would wed.

Is our destiny
forever the captive
of anticipation?
Will you claim me as your own?

You bring with you
the me who hides in your absence.
The me I would claim
as myself.

Hurry to me!
You are balm
        and softness.
        I am filled with kindness
                at the thought of you.

A love of such wonder
        requires great vigilance
        so that desire does not
                contrive away our rules.
                        Were it left un-bridled,
                        we would be consumed.

If there be a hint
        of divinity within me,
        may that divinity rise
                to the surface of my being
                        and strengthen me
                        in your view.

May I, in that moment
when our fires rise in fury,
turn you away from the anguish
of later regret.
Love yearned for is more pure
than love consummated.

Hurry to me!
I transcend to
my ethereal station
by your presence.
For now there is only
my waiting heart.

Gene Nay

Nancy's Kitchen

Well, here it comes, that crazy itchin'
to get right down to Nancy's Kitchen.

Nancy cooks and runs the show.
The rest pitch in to make things go.

Some folks come for "just good food,"
or to taste the happy mood.

There's always a smile and a warm "hello"
n'then a "thanks" when time to go.

Small and neat and really clean,
a nicer place you've never seen.

If you've looked you've already found
Nancy's food's the best in town.

The gals are charming and quick of wit.
They laugh and work and kid a bit.

Special is the way you feel,
    not just a body needin' a meal.

I'd tell you more, lots more but
    my stomach thinks my throats been cut.

Gotta feed this body, that'll stop this itchin'.
    Look out! I'm off to Nancy's Kitchen.

Gene Nay

natures' love

Midnight walks in quiet places
where dew drops lie on flower faces.

Rainy mist on forest trail,
tiny streams where leaves set sail.

Sunlit rays that light the hills
and warm the grass and daffodils.

Gulls that twist and soar above,
natures gentle signs of love.

All of these are free you see,
to people just like you and me,

if we allow our souls to feel
those things that more than we, are real.

Gene Nay

new dream

There's somethin' new in my life.
Didn't think it would ever come again,
not after the way I died last time.
That time I died so painfully,
I thought all feeling must be dead,
gone with my dream.

Now I have a new dream.
Impossible but true.
The purpose is there,
the zest for life,
the urge to create,
the need to accomplish,
a gentle one to live for.

Oh God, it's good to be alive!

Gene Nay

our love

The beginning was easy,
as it should be.
Our spirits light and breezy
as they could be.
There was no way of knowing
where it all was going,
but soon it would be showing
what it would be.

Ideas that seem to fit
like they should do.
Our words and talk gave wit
like they could do.
It seemed the time flew past,
the hours went so fast.
Had our fate been cast
to what it would do?

So quickly I perceived you,
as I should have.
Gentle face and spirit too,
as you could have.
Like ripples from a stone
into a puddle thrown,
had any ever known
what we would have?

The days and nights flashed by
with sunny skies above.
It seemed that we must try
to give romance a shove.
Faster and faster it went,
our minds so badly bent,
our faith to soon was spent
to recognize our love.

I was on the crest you see,
my joy was so grand.
You had lost the rest, I see,
you released my hand.
You had to get away.
I begged you so to stay,
endlessly I'd say,
"This love was planned."

The winds of time are kind
and this I now can see,
They softly whispered in my mind
that you still think of me.
Blooms, echoes, all I know,
Ripples, rapture, all will show,
that I need time to just let go
of thinking this *must* be.

Gene Nay

Why must hope
so often be
the servant
of despair?

perplexations

There is a stage
in the development of "loving,"
where the smallest irritation
becomes the largest annoyance.

It is further troubled
by the fact that at this point
one considers the relationship
beyond the preliminary precautions.

Being more relaxed
seems to have its' price.

As the need to be cautious passes,
with it often go the little things.

Things like "best foot forward,"
being considerate and protective
of each others feelings.

They seem to slip into the background.
as things like
taking for granted,
impatience and intolerance
loom up in the foreground.

Why is the cost of loving
so terribly high
for some?
How does one guard
against the changing values
that descend upon two people
as they become less sure
of each other?

The first step in finding a solution
is in recognizing the problem.

Gene Nay

pooch-a-rama

Life has now become so sweet,
thanks to Tiffany, Shane, and Pete.

Black n'brown, red and grey
are the colors of our day.

One is small and flits around,
another makes a thunder sound.

A third is more a type refined,
the grumpy one with stubbed behind.

They run, they play, jump and stomp,
sometimes sleep and often romp.

Now and then tempers flare
when at times it's hard to share.

Fill ’em up so they don’t pout,
then head’em up and move’em out.

“Let us out so we can potty,
and not catch heck for be’in naughty.”

“Open up cause now we’re back,
don’t you know we want our snack?”

One more spurt of runn’in round,
then they’re sleepy, n’settl’in down.

Dreamy snooze until the sun
and then another day of fun.

With yaps and wags it’s another day
of growls and leaps and rough-house play.

International dogs abound,
Mexican, French, and Irish hound.

Despite the trouble and time they take
the price is small for the joy they make.

Take it from me it's all worth while.
They give you a laugh, a tear, and a smile.

Creatures sent from heaven above
that come with an endless supply of love.

When you're down and life's a bog
return the kindness and love your dog.

Gene Nay

A human

loves you "if"

A dog

loves you "."

Poohlapooh

Poohlapooh,
the yummiyou,
tellya what
I think I'ldo

Think I'l make
A metalpig
n'teach'im how
ta'dance ajig.

N'if hisdanc'in
makes yasmile,
yullmay besit
witme awhile.

N'if yasit,
you yummiyou
I'll say I luvya
Poohlapooh!

Gene Nay

questions and answers

How can I tell you just what I feel
and make you aware of things I conceal?
All I can tell in my simple way
is you are my morning, my night and my day.

How can I show just how I care
when often my acts bring you despair?
All I can show to make myself clear,
is fumbling affections to show that you're dear.

How can I bring more comfort to you
when I confuse by things that I do?
All I can bring is joy, hope and pain,
for I'm just a man and so shall remain.

How can I make you know my need
and not seem selfish or tend to mislead?
All I can make you know of me
is just those things you are willing to see.

How can I change and not be blind
to things you do that are so kind?
All I can change I most surely will
as long as it helps our dreams to fulfill.

How can I be the love of your life,
when often I bring you sorrow and strife?
All I can be is just what I am,
sometimes I'm perfect, or not worth a damn.

How can I ask you never to go,
when I give you doubt and worry you so?
All I can ask is please, please stay,
for loosing your love is too much to pay.

How can I say what you are to me
or even hope to help you to see?
All I can say so you will know,
is you are my life and I love you so.

Gene Nay

reach

It looks so far
that little star.
Its tiny glow
just lets me know
that it's there.

So many things
have little strings
to help us see
just what can be
if we care.

They serve to teach
that we must reach,
for all we need
we'll have in deed,
if we dare.

Gene Nay

skeptics

The skeptics ploy,
add confusion.
Is all this joy
just illusion?

Voices calling.
A beckoned thought.
Petals falling,
the phrases caught.

Out of kilter,
not quite in phase.
Echoes filter
soft in the haze.

Doubtful voices
whisper sadly,
“Hasty choices
end so badly.”

So much advice
    and all so free.
        Who pay's the price?
    Just you and me.

I watched you fade,
    my eyes glistened.
        The choice was made,
    sad you listened.

What they decide
    gives you the blame.
        The skeptics hide
    behind your name.

Gene Nay

somewhere

Somewhere,
someone,
sometime again.

Faces,
spaces,
places I've been.

Tears,
fears,
years go by,

when
again
the yen to try?

Yet
I'll bet
I get the one,

and she
and me
will see the sun.

Fate
create
the great and small.

together
to weather
what ever may fall.

I'll
smile
a while for her,

somewhere,
someone,
sometime for sure.

Gene Nay

stewardess

A charming smile,
this lovely child,
if needed she'll be there.
Her gentle way
can make your day,
our princess of the air.

She lets you know
that she is so
like you would have her be.
She wins your trust
because she's just,
and acts with certainty.

She's always neat
and kind and sweet,
a lovely lady fair.
So thank the day
she comes your way
our princess of the air.

Gene Nay

Nothing can be
closer than two hearts,
yet at times it seems
the shortest distance
is the longest reach.

the child and the trees

Once I sat in deep despair
    On looking up a child was there.
He said, "What makes you feel so sad?
    Maybe I can make you glad."

I told the child, "Perhaps you can."
    So I smiled and then began,
"There are words that I have seen,
    wont you tell me what they mean?"

I asked the child, "What's bigotry?"
    He just smiled and said to me,
"Why that's a really giant tree
    that's bigger than the one you see."

I asked the child, "What's adult'ry?"
    Again he smiled, "Don't you see?
All along you should have known.
    That's a tree that's fully grown."

The thought took shape within my head,
    as I considerd all he'd said,
the worst of all grownup's disease
    is not seeing the forest for the trees.

Gene Nay

the danger there

I came to you so wounded,
so bruised with spirit bent.
I brought with me protection,
my walls made me content.
I found you too were wounded,
in need and feeling small.
We came together cautiously,
afraid to give our all.
As time went by it grew,
the love we learned to share.
Yet still we lingered, holding back,
we sensed the danger there.

The growing of togetherness
gave us a firm foundation.
We moved along and like a song
we harmonized creation.
The years began to tick away.
We grew in all we had.
With all the joy that we had found,
why was it we where sad?
It seemed that no one anywhere
could care the way we cared.
Yet still we lingered, holding back,
we sensed the danger there.

One of us from time to time
would act as not to try.
Feeling all the love inside
the other had to cry.
Doubts would rise, as walls came up
for safety and defense.
Could one of us be vulnerable
while one was on the fence?
The certainty of what we had
we obviously shared,
yet still we lingered, holding back,
we sensed the danger there.

And then it came, as sure it would,
the crisis, great and tall.
It swallowed us and tortured us.
Our dream began to fall.
Run away, find a haven,
give the mind a rest.
It must have been a fantasy.
No dream could face this test!
Let go the dream it's dead and gone!
Now we no longer care!
Yet still we linger, holding back,
we sense the danger there.

Looking back upon it all
I now can see so clearly.
It's not the crisis, but the walls
that's costing us so dearly.
If we had only let them down
when time was in our hand,
we'd never had to watch our dream
crumble into sand.
Our dream still lives, love of mine,
please face it if you dare!
The lingering, the holding back,
is all the danger there!

Gene Nay

the gentle need

So often through the days,
it's you I'm thinking of.
There are so many ways
to need the one you love.

If only you could know
the need I feel inside
I know you'd never go,
your heart would open wide.

I need the spark you give
whenever you are near.
You grant the will to live
and banish all my fear.

I need the things we share
and all the things we know,
the tender way you care
and how you love me so.

I need to hear you speak
the loving things you say.
The way you touch my cheek
to tell me, "It's okay."

I need your happy smile,
the rapture of your face.
The way that you beguile
when I'm in your embrace.

My body needs your touch,
it hungers for you so.
It seems I long so much
for what I've come to know.

I need your lovely mind
and how our souls can blend.
Our gentle thoughts are kind.
I hope they never end.

I need so much to see
the things I'm thinking of.
Know you'll always be
my gentle thoughts of love.

Gene Nay

the long road home

Gone is the sun,
the day's work is done,
and now the long road home.

Every house and tree,
familiar to me,
along the long road home.

Each hill and bend,
a passing friend
beside the long road home.

I work all day
so I can say,
at last the long road home.

Someone's sweet smile
makes all worthwhile
beyond the long road home.

If ever you were gone
I'd endlessly travel on
down that long, long road home.

Gene Nay

the most precious thing

You're part of my soul,
being with you makes me whole.

You're a constant image in my minds eye,
the thought of you is the pleasure of my sigh.

Your voice is the reward of my patient waiting,
for you're the purpose of all my creating.

Your touch is the realization that miracles exist,
where security is knowing it's me you've missed.

Your contentment is my souls caress,
the idea of you is my happiness.

Your sorrow is my grief,
you're the essence of my belief.

Your smile is my joy,
You're my angel envoy.

You're in my every waiting moment,
You're the healer of my disappointment.

Your least pleasure is my delight,
your warmth is my sunlight.

You're a haunting fragrance of a flowered dream,
your spirit hovers like wisps of moonbeam.

You're the source of my times of loneliness,
and my aching need to give tenderness.

Your existence is my inner sanctum,
granting me strength to overcome.

Your kindness is a treasure for us,
your laughter is my celestial chorus.

You inspire my sensitivity,
You're my only archway to tranquility.

The most precious thing I'll ever know
is the painful joy of loving you so.

Gene Nay

the pledge

I pledge to you a solemn vow
to love you tomorrow more than now.
I pledge that I shall always be
the kind of man you'll wish to see.
I pledge that I will never use you
or in anyway abuse you.
I pledge to share my nights and days
and fill our lives with gentle ways.
I pledge that I will let you live
and take but what you wish to give.
I pledge to taste your smiles and tears,
to give you joy and calm your fears.
I pledge that I shall truly teach you
that most of all I wish to reach you.
I pledge that I shall rearrange
the things in me you wish to change.
I pledge I'll place no other above you
for God Himself has sent me to love you.

Gene Nay

the quiet of the night

There's a peace that comes to me
in the quiet of the night,
when I close my eyes to see
your arms around me tight.

I know it's only make believe
and yet it seems so real.
One may think that I deceive
and force myself to feel.

It's not at all like that to me,
the memories are fresh.
So vivid are the things I see,
I even feel your flesh.

The scent of you still lingers,
    the warmth of you is there.
The feeling of your fingers
    and softness of your hair.

Most of all I hear your voice
    and gentle things you say.
That's why you'll always be my choice
    and in my heart you'll stay.

When our day comes, I know it's true
    you'll see that I was right
to close my eyes and live with you
    in the quiet of the night.

Gene Nay

the Moose Lodge Dance

I thought I'd take a chance
and catch the Moose Lodge dance.

People talking,
some with smiles.
Good times for most,
sad times for some.

Glasses up, glasses down.
Dancing feet, a shuffle sound.

Saturday night dance,
what a sight!
A real live band!
The Moose are loose tonight!

Music fast, music slow.
Some folks come, some go.

Together girls are dancin'.
Where are the boys?

Some are thin, some are round.
Stamping feet upon the ground.
A happy sound.

A tiny girl spinning, jumping,
sister thumping.

Chatter, chatter everywhere.

Now the little girl is on the bandstand,
mike in hand, singin' so grand.

"Superman to the rescue."

"Funny Face," many faces,
a happy sadness held in traces.

Dresses, jeans, slacks, shorts,
fancy, plain, all sorts.
Tennis shoes, sandals, boots,
cowboy clothes, and business suits.

She says, "Yes"! He says, "No"!
Yet the coward wants to so.
Dancin's all in fun.

Some are leanin' on the bar,
others headin' for the car.
The little girl's a singin' star.
How grand they all are.

Peaceful,
happy,
good times
for most.

Our
antlered
friend
is host

Curious thoughts,
ladies talk,
pretty faces.

What hides
behind the eyes?
Fathomless mysteries,
obvious simplicities.

Why stop this description now?
Just to let the high point carry.

Gene Nay

the time

The time has come,
at long last,
to let the old go by.

I'll cast aside
what's gone past.
and let the memories die.

Just letting go,
the glad times
is not an easy thing.

It seems to me
that sad rhymes
still want so much to cling.

Yet now I have
a good chance
for life to bring to bear

it's sunny side,
a lovely dance
all filled with love and care.

Gene Nay

things unseen

Everyone should have somewhere
to lay each burden, every care,
tasting restful quiet moments
and never need despair
for things unseen.

Yet few will think to look within
to find the place where dreams begin.
Will they find no peaceful moments
or words that mean "I win"
from things unseen?

What strange creatures man must be
with open eyes that seldom see
that in his mind, the best moments
like the best things are free,
as things unseen.

That special place is yours my friend,
a place where good things never end,
where you can hold precious moments
that will forever lend
grand things unseen.

Deep within there lies a place
of solitude and peaceful grace.
It's there I seek private moments
to contemplate and face
those things unseen.

Seldom I let others look
or make myself an open book,
laying bare unspoken moments,
wherein my soul partook
of things unseen.

Can you picture in your mind
a haven where you always find
quiet, peaceful, simple moments,
worldly woes far behind
most things unseen?

Loosened shackles all let go
that your mind may soar and know
contented joy, happy moments,
loving seeds that will sew
nice things unseen.

May I grant you this one thing
        that your heart and soul take wing.
In the best of gentle moments
        may your life always bring
                good things unseen.

When your daydreams do come true
        remember their a gift from you.
You'll within your quiet moments
        capture what you pursue
                in things unseen.

Gene Nay

today then tomorrow

God sent us His son,
the only pure one,
to pay for our sins great and small.

This gift from above
granted each one His love
and cleansed the sin from us all.

I had been so bad
in the evil I had,
my guilt piled high on the shelf.

Now it's all gone,
I can carry on,
He's taken it all on Himself.

He laid down His life,
          took all of my strife
and gave me a peace deep inside.

For it was His plan
          to suffer for man.
He suffered, He bled, and He died.

Now that I know
          I can let it all go,
the guilt, the hurt, and the sorrow.

It's safe to begin,
          He's taken my sin.
No more past, just today then tomorrow.

Gene Nay

truck stop

There's a blessed site,
when you're haulin' a load.
Truck stop on the right,
three miles up the road.

Stiff and sore
from fightin' this rig.
Two miles more.
The sign's so big.

Check the right
rear inside.
Lord this night's
a hell'uva ride.

I'll just grab
some eggs'n grits.
Get out'a this cab,
it's give'n me fits.

Bright light gleams
    a mile away.
Catch some dreams
    and hit the hay.

Years go by
    and every day
want'a try
    n'easier way.

Somethin' 'bout
    runnin' the road
makes me doubt
    I'll ever unload

this rig o'mine,
    it's part of me.
It runs so fine!
    And now I see

the lights ahead.
        I'll have some chow.
Lord I'm dead.
        Eat n'sleep now.

Prettiest site
        I'll ever see,
Truck Stop turn right
        in front of me.

Gene Nay

true love

Of all the treasures
in all God's worlds
and all His skies above,

lifes greatest gift,
most precious gem,
is that we call true love.

I've searched the world
and I can see,
the answer now is clear to me,

the price at which
true love is bought
is just to . . .

. . . *hold a gentle thought.*

Gene Nay

yours for the taking

Where are the things that I so want to say?
Soon as I see you they all go away.
They're all in my mind and so crystal clear,
but all of them fade the moment you're near.

My plans and dreams that are aching to start,
can't be expressed until after we part.
Suffer we do from crosses we carry.
Crosses that we would so like to bury.

If I bring to your lips a soul felt smile,
I'm sure you will heal and after a while,
the things you've needed for so long to see,
yours for the taking, just take them from me.

Gene Nay

will there be?

Will there be a special one
to walk with me through rain and sun
and find the end that we've begun.

Let me fill our nights and days
with happy times and easy ways
to guide us past the clear and haze.

Hand in hand we both will go
to where the balmy breezes blow
and we shall watch our flowers grow.

Beneath the pines by riverside,
where in the clouds the mountains hide,
who's waters to the ocean glide.

Where deer and elk and game abound
with natures bounty all around
a future for us can be found.

A brand new life for us to share.
We'll leave behind our worldly care
and speak to God in whispered prayer.

Gene Nay

More than the
ability to speak
give me something
worthwhile to say.

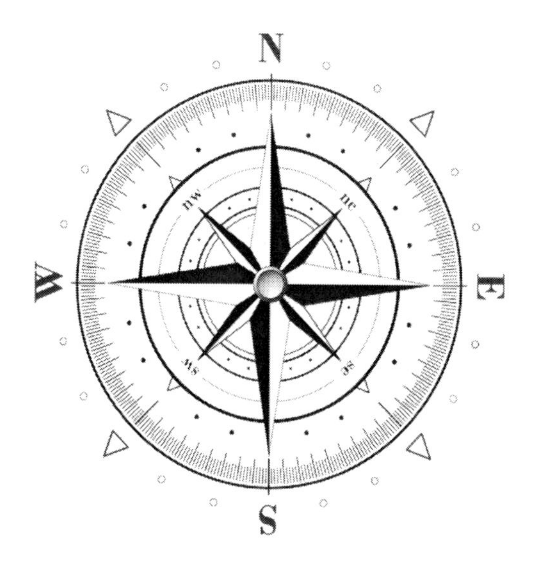

Section 3 Stories, Talks & Experiences

beyond communication

(a true story)

I have always been able to communicate well with most people. To a large extent my life's specialty has been primarily along these lines. There was a time, many years ago, when it went way beyond normal communication. Are you skeptical about ESP, (Extra Sensory Perception)? I'm not, not anymore.

In the early seventies I had a job assignment in Seattle. It was late June of an absolutely beautiful summer. Have you ever been there? If you have, you already know. If you haven't, make it a point, you owe it to yourself to see it. Take a ferry-boat ride out to Bremerton. Sit out on the top deck and take it all in. Blue sky, white clouds, blue-er water, green trees, golden shoreline, pines growing right down into the water. A setting painted by the master artist himself, and all lit up by the most glorious sun you've ever seen. Air conditioned by a balmy breeze and of course, the finishing touch, someone wonderful to share it with. I was lucky, I had a wonderful friend named Judy, and Judy and I had *communication!*

Judy worked at the hotel where I stayed in Seattle. We were good friends and could almost read each others thoughts. It was spooky at times. Judy opened the door to a world of communication that had never before existed.

One afternoon as I was driving by the hotel, I saw her car parked in the restaurant parking area. On an impulse I decided to leave a cryptic little message on her windshield. We were planning to get together for supper that night, so I thought a note might be fun. It read; "Who knows what lies in the heart of Judy? The Phantom knows!" I knew she'd like it and I smiled to myself as I drove away. At supper she told me how she had enjoyed receiving it.

Time went by and my job in Seattle came to an end. Judy drove me to the airport to see me off and as we parted we promised to keep in touch with each other. That's when some really strange things began to happen.

I had changed job assaignments and my travels now took me to several cities on a speaking tour. It seemed like I spent more time in the air than on the ground. Every time I got on a plane, one of three things happened. Either the crew just came from Seattle, or they would end their flight schedule there, and a Seattle newspaper would be waiting on the seat that I had selected at the ticket counter. Not just once, but every time. We did keep in touch. Every time I was troubled, Judy would know somehow and I would either get a letter or a phone call. I somehow knew when things were'nt going well for her and I would get this overwhelming compulsion to call or write to her. Neither of us had to be told when, we just knew. For many months this strange long distance comfort was always there whenever it was needed.

One day, as my plane rose up out of the clouds over Salt Lake City, an unusual sight sprang at me from my window. I looked out on a huge cloud valley with the sun at the other end shining and highlighting the billowy and craggy cloud precipices. It was a glorious sight, and a sensitive picture. I suddenly felt compelled to write a letter to Judy, my dear friend was in trouble and somehow I knew it . I had to write words of reassurance and encouragement. When the plane made its' stop over in Las Vegas I mailed the letter. I strongly felt that it would help.

Three nights later, after my speech, I was sitting in the lounge talking to some friends and enjoying the music of a wonderful Hawaiian band. Suddenly out of the blue I said, "I have to go to my room you guys." I walked out right in the middle of our conversation.

Unknown to me, Judy had for some time been involved in a relationship that had turned very sour and things were going very badly for her. That evening she had ran to her car in a state of hysteria, with but one thought in mind. She was going to drive her car right off a bridge that was under construction and currently ended in mid air about a hundred and fifty feet above the ocean. She felt there was no other way out. As she flung open her car door, a forgotten note fluttered down from over her visor. It read; "Who knows what lurks in the heart of Judy? The Phantom knows." She immediately drove home, opened her mailbox for the first time in days, and right there on top of the stack of ignored mail sat a letter post marked from Las Vegas. She opened the letter, read it, and went straight to her telephone.

I had forgotten my bewildered friends in the lounge by the time I reached my room. I opened the door, stepped toward the phone, put my hand on it just as it rang, picked it up, and before she spoke, I said, "Hi Judy." The other end was very quiet for a moment and then I heard her say softly, "Wow!"

Coincidence? I hardly think so. We lost touch many years ago, but the experience is very much alive in my mind. The most important thing between us was a gentle knowing of each other. What ever our link was it was far beyond what is usually considered as communication. Who could have guessed that a simple gesture of friendship and fun would save the life of someone I still carry among my most precious memories. There really are times when we may be called to be someones angel. I know this to be true and I am pleased to share this experience with you.

Gene Nay

The hard

and reluctant awakening

that comes when you

lay down your

opinions, premonitions,

fantasies, and suspicions,

and pickup naked reality.

Dear Kenny, Faith, and family,

(a true story)

For over a year now everyone I love has left. Now two very special people are about to leave too. I'm really tired of tail lights, out of town flights, and goodby's. It's lucky for you that I don't just follow you. I would too, but the Polly Anna in me say's, "What if someone who left decides to come back?" It'd be just my luck and I wouldn't be here to even know it! So I guess I'm here to stay. Be of good cheer though, I don't have anyone else who can leave. Here's my tribute to:

Kenny & Faith

Kenny is a gentleman, a nice guy
a sentimental man, a comedy high.
Faith is a pleaser, a nice girl,
a real squeezer, a dancin' whirl.

They make you smile. They make you think.
They'll tease a while, and give a wink.
I know I'll feel they're just out of sight.
won't be real on Saturday night.

One day you'll see, they're gonna visit
to see you and me and whoever isit?
It'll be so great, you'll see then.
I just can't wait, to see'em again.

Noise and clatter! A Martian attack?
All that chatter. It's them and their back!
Just take my word, the poet sayeth
it's the thunderin' herd and Kenny and Fay-eth!

Please know, our dear friends, you will be missed more than you can guess. The void you leave behind will be very hard to fill. It will leave us who remain to seek comfort from each other as best we can. We know the Lord has something special in mind for you and it must be very important. He would never take you away from us were it not. You have our fondest wishes that you will be blessed with wonderfull opportunities to grow and serve the Lord. Think of it, a whole new life and someone to share it with. Perhaps you have all the blessings you'll ever need.

Love and happiness to you all,

Gene Nay

Mother's Day

(a true story)

My first talk since I ecclesiastically vanished into obscurity in 1961 was at the New River Branch of the Deer Valley Stake on Mother's day 1989. At that time it had been about thirty years since I had spoken in church. Because this talk was a tribute to a very special and dear friend, I decided to pay that tribute once more in 1993. Incidentally, because of this special mom, I met a collection of very unusual mothers. In life we discover that many things are not quite what they seem. Our viewpoint makes the difference. As an example consider the following:

the child and the trees

Once I sat in deep despair.
    On looking up a child was there.
He said, "What makes you feel so sad?
    Maybe I can make you glad."

I told the child, "Perhaps you can."
    So I smiled and then began,
"There are words that I have seen,
    wont you tell me what they mean?"

I asked the child, "What's bigotry?"
He just smiled and said to me,
"Why that's a really giant tree
that's bigger than the one you see."

I asked the child, "What's adult'ry?"
Again he smiled, "Don't you see?
All along you should have known.
That's a tree that's fully grown."

The thought took shape within my head,
as I considerd all he'd said,
the worst of all grownups disease
is not seeing the forest for the trees.

Gene Nay

Yes, many things are not what they seem, and least of all mothers. They are all full of surprises. Take for example, my friend Tish. You'd think she's just an ordinary, normal, everyday "mom", but I can assure you she's anything but ordinary, or everyday and the word "normal" just doesn't apply.

If she invites you to go for a walk you had better be prepared. Here's her idea of a walk. She says, "I'm taking you to my special place. Do you see the mesa over there? That's where we're walking to." You say, "Oh, this mesa?" Then Tish tells you, "Oh no, that one, waaaay over there!"

You arrive at the base of the mesa, in what seems like a day or two, to stare up at what looks like a long lost arm of the continental divide, and say, "Now what?" Tish calmly announces, "Up!" Well it looked like the very definition of the word. "I'm taking you up the south side. It's a little steeper, but it's quicker." It was kind of like a trip to the top of the Empire State Building, on a day when the elevators are out of service.

"Walk and not be weary, run and not feint. For me it was more like sit down before you pass out! I can tell you that when Tish observes the word of wisdom, it pays off big time!!

It was a grueling climb to the top and the view was worth the pain. The valleys below us were magnificent, but why did every mesquite fly in the world have to live on this mesa? Their accuracy is incredible. What other creature can navigate so well at ninety miles an hour that they can fly directly into an opening no larger than a nostril! Let us remember though, they too are creations of Heavenly Father and some of them are mothers, and today is their day too!

Mothers aren't always recognizable. We found mother-to-be desert tortoise, which Tish had returned to the mesa on an earlier visit. In a lovely new home with a view, that had freshly been excavated, she was preparing for the early summer arrival of her shell clad offspring. Like any mother, she had chosen her site with great care and an eye single to the safety of her coming family.

Tish told of a coyote she had once encountered on a previous excursion to the site. The animals behavior was very peculiar. Running ahead of her, it bounded sideways in plain view. It would stop momentarily and then bound away again, exposing it's opposite flank. A gestures designed by the instinctive mind of a creature designed by the creative hand of our Heavenly Father. A gesture which draws danger to herself and away from her puppy laden den. No indeed, mother's aren't always what they seem.

On top of the mesa, not visible from below, is a remarkable Indian ruin. All that is still standing are the walls of stone. Each wall is pilled precisely in two rows of stones, tapered toward the centerline so that each half of the wall leaned against its counterpart. Simple, secure, and still standing five hundred to a thousand years later, and believe it or not without mortar. I wondered what a home, built to today's construction standards, would look like after the same amount of time?

If you listen quietly you can hear the whispering of memories echoing softly on the wind that rustles through the palo verde trees, then moans low through the walls of stone. Children played here. People laughed and wept, lived and died. The highlights of their existence are etched in the petro glyphs on the larger boulders that dot the outer perimeter of the encampment. Pictures of goats, bighorn sheep, deer, people, and even infant sized foot prints. Someone should have told the artist that drew a rider on horseback, there were no horses in the Americas until the Spaniards brought them here, according to the experts. Of course few of the experts ever read the Book of Mormon so how could they know. After sometime of site-seeing and exploring it was time to head down off the mesa. Tish said, "We'll go down the north side. It's longer but easier." I should have told her that if we just jumped off the south side we could be half way home by the time we hit the ground!

Sometimes it's hard to notice a mother not being what she seems. As we came to the bottom of the slope below the mesa and wound our way between the trees and cactus, you could feel those big brown eyes guardedly watching. The protective nature of motherhood is as subtle as the range cow I observed interposing herself between us and her calf as we passed by. It seemed to me that this creature of God was naturally endowed with some of the same values and concerns as its divine creator.

We took a breather at Fig Springs, splashed water on our faces, and it felt mighty refreshing. There are both figs and springs there in case you've wondered, then we pushed off again. Home, ... I knew it was out there somewhere! Tish lead the way at what felt like a near gallop. How remarkable she is. Incredible stamina and a natural teacher. She knows a million interesting things, but how she managed to "Run without feinting" and talk about them all at the same time was bewildering. Her chatter was a tapestry all interwoven with facts and tidbits of history, geology, and archaeology. This mother is also the perfect tour guide. She had no idea how much sharing her special place meant to me.

The most beautiful part of the whole trip was the sharing of her feelings about church and her family. Here is a mom who struggles to survive her scars and her heartbreak, and loves her family, her church, and her motherhood.

Along the way home the evidence of just what a hike this really had been came to light when we passed the Texas state line . . . . twice. Perhaps it was just hallucinatory exhaustion. Things were just a bit blurry by then.

It had been an experience I certainly will long treasure. A day filled with wonderful examples of motherhood. Creatures great and small doing what Heavenly Father intended. Serving, protecting, teaching, and providing for their own.

How strange it was to discover so many shared qualities between the animal kingdom and the world of the human mother. Tish has the persistence and stamina of the mesquite fly, the ingenuity and determination of the desert tortoise, and the caring and protective nature of the coyote and the range cow. Add to this the warmth and kindness of human fellowship, and you have a mother that is fun, safe, and comfortable to be with, and her name is Tish.

I cannot think of Mother's Day without thinking of Tish. Once again she is my tribute to Mother's Day. It's an honor to know and call her friend. I salute her and I know the Lord smiles upon her. Happy Mother's Day to Tish and to all mothers. I bear this testimony to all present and to our Lord Jesus Christ. Amen.

Gene Nay

He said,
"I've only made one mistake
in my whole life.
That was when
I thought I was wrong,
but I wasn't."

July 24th, 1849

(almost pure fiction)

The celebration had begun, and Brother Brigham was already worn out. He thought to himself, "Being a prophet is hard work, but being a husband to 27 wives is absolutely exhausting." Of course 56 children would make most men run screaming into the mountains never to return.

It is well to remember that Brother Brigham, as he was most often referred to, was very much an ordinary man as well as an extraordinary man. His good friend, Sleeping Bear, Chief of one of the local Ute Indian tribes, and frequent attending celebrity to many of the local functions, was always looking for an opportunity to pull some kind of wild and silly shenanigan on the Prophet. No one knew who would get the worst of the deal, but all knew that something was bound to happen before the revelry was over. Most were betting on Brother Brigham because of his great inspiration. Others were saying, "Oh no, Sleeping Bear owes him one, and he's sure to get even."

As the day wore on and the meal was served the tension in the crowd mounted. Seated just across from each other, and waiting for a long winded speaker to conclude his liturgy, the old Indian had nodded off, and Brigham exhaled with a sigh of relief. Now he could relax. He looked at the beautiful pecan pie that had been placed in front of him, it was rumored to be his favorite and had been especially prepared for him by wife number 13, or was it 23, he was so tired and the truth was the pie was always rather like glue. Of course he would know enough to "oooh and aaahh" in delight when eating it. He thought to himself, "Is Brother Pratt ever going to quit prattling on so I can eat this pie and go home and take a nap?"

With his head turned to the side as if listening intently, Brother Brigham slowly leaned more and more forward as Brother Pratt droned on. It was precisely at the moment when the prophets head was sinking toward the surface of that very sticky pie that the old Indians' left eye popped open. No, he had not been sleeping, he had been waiting, and now opportunity was his. Reaching across the table, he gently put his hand on the side of the prophets face and firmly helped him to settle his weary head into the "pecan pillow" that had patiently cooled as it waited for him there. Oh the comfort, the smell, the sweetness, oh the stickiness, oh the glue, and the sudden gasp and silence of the crowd. The prophets' head snapped up only to see the empty pie dish sitting on the table before him. He was totally unaware of the gooey glob stuck to the side of his head. In his sleepy disorientation he blurted out, "What day is this?"

Brother Brigham should never have asked the question. A sly smile slid across Sleeping Bears face. Now he claimed his victory. With great chiefly authority he answered in the immortal words we still celebrate a century and a half later. "It's pie on ear day!"

Gene Nay

Let me realize
my loss
when I refuse to serve.

the incredible power of a single flower

(a true story)

I very much enjoyed speaking at the Disneyland Hotel in Anaheim, California. It's kind of a world unto itself. I'm not referring to the amusement park. Everyone knows what a wonderful place that is. I'm speaking of the Hotel complex. It's made up of a fabulous concoction of stores, shops, restaurants, lounges, gardens, artificial harbors, dancing waters, colors, lights, sunshine, and it is all very captivating. I wonder how many of the guests miss the magic that's right there in front of them in their haste to get across the street to the theme park.

I had a good deal of idle time while I was there and so I made the Hotel complex my main attraction, rather than join the race to the monorail. I've always hated the thought of just being another member of the herd. I let the cattle stampede on by in their quest for thrilling rides and just took a walk through the gardens and shops.

I had become slightly acquainted with a lady in an apparel shop. She had a lovely smile that made you feel so comfortable. I've always wondered how she did that. Her name was Sue and she had the most pleasant sincerity. Sue loved flowers, one at a time. It was through her that the meaning of flower power was soon to be driven home in me.

Sue is such a kind, gentle and loving person. A good friend. She made me aware of my own insensitivity in a most agreeable way. I had always considered myself a sensitive person. To discover that I wasn't the kind of person that I had thought myself to be was most unsettling. She had the ability to make you look within yourself and I hadn't liked what I had seen. It is possible to change yourself though, if you really wish to. She made me want that.

One day as I was on my way down to see Sue, a thought occurred to me. Our little talks had become the highlight of my day. I felt strangely compelled to take her a single flower. Now of course, flowers at the Disneyland Hotel are as numerous as the sand at the seashore and jealously guarded by the hotel security people who are everywhere. My every attempt at picking one was thwarted by some watchful eye. Finally I gave up in despair rather than miss our short visit. I walked over to the counter and without a word being spoken, she reached down then stood up and handed me a single flower. I found myself softly saying, "Wow!" I had looked high and low for just one flower and here it was, handed to me. Our ritual had begun, always a flower.

Sue and I would talk at great length about life, love, happiness, and philosophy. Once she asked me, "What do you seek from a woman?" She wanted to hear me express in the strictest terms exactly what kind of person my ideal woman must be. She didn't want a spontaneous answer. Nothing off of the top of my head would do. She wanted me to state it exactly. I told her I would write it out that night. I had thought I would just dash off a few lines and that it wouldn't be a problem. I started that evening at 10:00pm. When I finished I was nearly up to my knees in crumpled paper and it was 4:00 a.m. It was not my first attempt at writing. I had written lesson plans and many sales and promotional presentations for years. It was however, my first attempt at describing such a personal opinion. When I finally finished I knew instantly that it was exactly how I felt. It read:

I seek from my Lady . . . .

an intimate intellectual relationship.
One in which the inner truths
of our beings can unite
and fully appreciate each other.

The joys of learning to know
and accept our differences
and to have more because of them.

To be able to communicate
on any subject, at any depth,
for any length of time,
without misgivings, regrets, or shame.

To be able to be
natural and yet be concerned.

To be able to be intimate
without being physical.

To be able to be loved
without making love.

To make love
without demanding love.

To be above all
honest, gentle, understanding, appreciative
and compassionate with each other.

To taste of each others cup,
leaving us both richer for the tasting.

Thus fulfilling our mutual needs.

Gene Nay

One morning, when I stopped in to see Sue, she gave me a yellow daisy and said, "Find someone who needs it." For the first time I was to see the beautiful and the difficult aspects of "flower power."

Let me make it perfectly clear that I am a businessman, not a hippie freak. Could I picture myself carrying this stupid flower around trying to give it to someone? No way! Not me! My mind just slammed shut. Then she said, "Someone will truly need it just as you do now." Well, it was true, I had a problem confront me earlier that I hadn't mentioned and I must confess I was really looking forward to her gentle words and the flower she would have for me. I decided that the little flower she had just given me should have a chance to do its work for someone else just as it had for me. I mean what difference could it make if I carried a flower around. So I had a flower in my hand. So I looked a little silly. So what?

I was now curious as to whether the little blossoms magic was all used up or not anyway. All the rest of the day I carried the little yellow bloom. Twice I started to approach people who looked to be in some sort of distress, but some sign of insensitivity in them warned me off. That evening I gave my presentation, picked up my wilting daisy and marched out to continue the search for that someone who really needed it. I guess I'm making myself sound a little like Don Quixote, however that's not how I felt. I was simply going to continue the experiment and see what happened.

I'm a nut for good music and many of the Hotels and larger motels in the Disneyland area have great restaurants and excellent entertainment. So I hopped from show to show and bowling alleys to bus stations. Anywhere there were people. I thought of the amusement park and decided I probably couldn't study the reaction of the receiver. Disgruntled and dejected I trudged back to the motel restaurant & lounge. I visited with some of my business associates there who had been enjoying the good food and fine music. I sat down with them and looked over the crowd. I almost gave the flower to a waitress as they began closing up but something said no. The flower was wilting fast now and I was already dreading the report I would have for my friend Sue in the morning. As I stepped out the door and headed toward my room I noticed someone was walking straight at me with his eyes fixed on my flower. It was Dave, the day time desk clerk and I could see trouble all over his face. His first words were, "Do you need that flower?" To myself I said, "Wow." Then I noticed Dave's girlfriend was sitting in his car with tears streaming down her face. She was from Australia and was going to school here. Her folks had gotten wind of their plans to marry and had sent orders for her to return home immediately. I told Dave I had been looking all day for the person who really needed it. He took the flower, got back into the car and when she opened her tearful eyes the flower was all she could see. When I saw her smile through all those tears I knew that no one would ever convince me that there is no such thing as "flower power." As for Dave and his lady, they were soon married and living in Australia.

What was the magic of the flower? Maybe empathy. True empathy in my opinion is the closest thing to ESP that most people can experience. I believe the reason flowers were put here is to remind us to put ourselves in the other persons shoes before we pass judgment on them. Flowers are a gift, another illustration of a loving Heavenly Father.

Gene Nay

about prejudice

Easter Sunrise Service

(a true story)

It was still quite dark upon arrival in a little southwestern town where I had been invited to be one of several speakers at their annual Easter Sunrise Services. It was the custom of the City Fathers to select a dozen or so churches and have them send a representative to give a brief talk on a subject of their choice. The many neighborhood Christian churches considered it quite an honor to be selected to speak at this event that was held each year at the Community Park. I accepted that opportunity immediately because I had heard that the three most prominent clergymen in this very small city had refused to speak and even decided to boycott the meeting when they heard that a Mormon was going to be one of the speakers. Having been so advised I had decided to speak on prejudice and so I began:

"Easter morning we celebrate the overcoming of physical death, through our beloved Lord's resurrection. When I think of what an incredible gift this was for the Savior to provide for all of us, I ask myself what can I give you in about four minutes that would be a worth while Easter gift. In these days when hate and prejudice run rampant through our society it would be nice to share in some of the dignity, love and respect that exists between an eleven year old boy and his minister. I've titled this poem:

Charlie and the Reverend

Charlie was a curious boy
and hungered so to learn.
Heaven, he'd heard, is full of joy
and hell a place to burn.

He had so many questions on
the things that preachers say.
Today we live, tomorrow we're gone.
Will we collect or pay?

He had to know what lay ahead,
and so he so he sought the truth
and cornered Reverend Halared
behind the preachers booth.

"Please dear Reverend tell me now,
though I'm just eleven,
what's it like, if some how
I should go to Heaven?"

Said the Reverend, "Now don't you worry,
you're just a youth, you see."
Poor Charlie's hands waived in a flurry,
"But I've asked you seriously."

The Reverend saw the boy had meant it
when he had made his plea.
Sensing Charlie might resent it
he said, "Now let me see.

You want to know what Heaven's about,
and that's alright with me.
You needn't fret or ever doubt
it's quite the place to be.

Heaven's a wondrous and joyful place
with streets of gold and jewels,
where God can live and show His face
and never deal with fools.

It's filled with music forever more,
sweet songs of praise for our King,
with nothing to want or hunger for
forever well sing and sing."

The Reverend had told what he believed
and told it straight and truly,
but Charlie seemed so unrelieved
as though he'd been treated cruelly.

How could the child be so disappointed,
the Reverend wanted to know.
To gaze forever upon the Anointed
would please the Reverend so.

The Reverend couldn't comprehend it
and said, "Please Charlie, sit down.
Heaven is God's, I didn't invent it.
Why doe's it make you frown?"

Charlie sat down and sadly said,
"How could I have been so wrong?
I've always felt that when we are dead
There'd be more to Heaven than song.

I pictured a home, a place of my own
with endless things to do,
where I could let the God I've known
teach me just like you.

I thought of myself all big and grown up,
learning what God likes to do.
Visions of trees and flowers sown up
in ways that He only knew.

I dreamed of suns and planets and stars
like those I see in the sky,
of shaping and placing the nears and the fars
under Fathers watchful eye.

It hurts me to think that He'd spend His days
and want nothing more to do
than listen to praise and songs and hoorays
from all and from me and from you.

I thought He would share and teach us to care
and tell us of secrets He knows.
It seems He'd want more than for us to stare
at His face and His throne and His clothes.

I'm so sorry sir, but the Heaven you know
is not what I had hoped for.
I must admit that I thought He'd show
how to do things and much more.

I see I was wrong and I hope He'll forgive.
My folly is that of my age.
Now that it's clear, as long as I live,
I'll sing to Him page after page.

When I get there I'll know all the songs,
especially those He likes best.
I'm sure I'll feel I'm where I belong
and that I'm so truly blessed.

Thank you Reverend for all your advice.
You've been so helpful to me.
I'll study real hard and sing so nice.
I'll make Him so proud, you'll see."

"Charlie's a man now," said Reverend Halared
as the boy slowly walked away.
"He's let go the dreams that filled his head.
Reality will now bear sway.

Why it sounded like the boy had believed
he'd become like God above."
The grateful Reverend was so relieved.
He had straightened him out with love.

Still something in what the child had said,
had made the Reverend recall,
words of the Savior spoke in his head.
could he remember it all?

In Romans 8 it seems like I read,
"We're children of God and His heirs."
Revelations 21, he remembered it said.
"He that overcomes all is theirs."

The Reverends hand was searching to find
the switch to turn out the light.
"Have I just snuffed the light in his mind?
Could it be the boy had been right?"

Gene Nay

Please Lord, soften the hearts of those of us who minister in thy service. Especially those who find fault with others beliefs and their doctrine. Bless us that we might love each other in spite of our differences. Let us not make a mockery of our Lord's great pain and sacrifice by harboring prejudice. Let us not be blinded to the good fruits of each others labors. Open our hearts to the love of Christ that we are ordained to feel for each other. Help us to realize that though we have some differences we also have many significant "same's." May those "same's" be the force which binds us together in the service of our Lord, and may our differences be our golden opportunity to set prejudice aside.

I concluded my talk in the Lord's name and watched as a few of the following preachers assured the crowd that the poetic points I had made wouldn't be found anywhere in the Bible. The Apostles Paul and John wouldn't have been very happy to hear that. Neither would Jesus for whom they spoke.

I was more than pleased by the number of people who told me that my talk was exactly how they had pictured Heaven themselves. So many had enjoyed my little talk and said, "Be sure and come back and speak at our next Easter Sunrise Service." "I'd be more than happy to" I told them, but somehow the invitation never arrived. I wonder what those preachers will do now that the Mormons are planning to build a chapel right there in town. I hope it's soon, I'm planning another talk on "Perseverance."

A few years later I met a person from that small town who had attended that Easter Morning service. He told me that within ninety days of my talk all three of the boycotting ministers had been asked to leave by their own congregations.

Gene Nay

humility

(a true story)

When I was a young man of seventeen I was deeply involved with my religeon. I had joined the church after gaining a testimony of its' truth and this was the result of the efforts of young men I came to know through attending Redondo Union High School in Redondo Beach, California.

Later in my 19th summer I had an experience that was to be one of my lifes greatest lessons. This incident also marked a turning point in my spiritual existence that I would fail to recognize for many years. At that time I worked for my father in the San Fernando Valley in southern California. Dad had a soft ice cream store on Sepulveda Boulevard. He also had several jeeps with freezer boxes on them for street vending. Behind the store there were some large freezers which were locked up every night with chains and large padlocks to prevent theft. The keys were a constant source of headaches to dad. Loosing the keys himself caused him great irritation. I was very glad that I had never commited that crime myself.

I remember one day when my father, a big man, was on a near rampage after paying what he thought was a ransome for once again replacing all the keys in the place.

As he handed me a new set, I remember he scowled and said, "I'll work you over if you loose these." From the way he stalked off I was certain he would make his threat good. I don't mean to make him sound as though he handed out regular beatings, that was not the case. Dad and I had very fews physical encounters. Dad was a bully though and tended to take his frustrations out on others, even if he was at fault.

I had loaded up the jeep with all the ice cream I thought I could sell that day, and as I got out toward Reseda I heard someone honk behind me. It was a warm day and someone was ready for ice cream. I pulled off to the side of the road, got out, unlocked the box, put the lock and keys on top of the truck, filled their order, collected their money, and said to myself, "It's going to be a great day for selling ice cream, it's really getting hot!"

Upon arriving at the starting point of my route I stopped the truck and prepared to unlock it for the day's business. I reached for the keys and they were not were they belonged. PANIC! They were gone! A large ring that had probably 20 to 30 keys on it. Where were they? I searched the cab frantically, but to no avail. Mentally I retraced every move I had made since leaving the store right up to the point when I heard the honk from behind. Then I knew. I had left them on top of the truck while I sold that first order. I could even see them in my mind with one of the keys plugged into the padlock resting just above my head on top of the truck freezer box as I had reached in to pick out my customers order. The lock was about 2 by 3 by 1 inch in size. The key ring was a piece of heavy copper wire six inches in diameter on which the keys all hung. I dared to hope for only a moment as I jumped out of the truck. Then I discovered what I already knew, there was nothing on top of the truck.

My mind was racing. I envisioned every inch of the road from the time I stopped for that first sale to the point where I was then. Many miles of left and right turns. To say nothing of the bumps and dips. How would I ever find them. What if someone had just picked them up? I experienced the feeling of utter hopelessness.

I had the habit of prayer at that time and I knew that the Lord was the only one who could help me. I had no doubt that he could, only would he? I remember how upset I was and how sincere my plea for help had been. As I sat there in the jeep a picture of an intersection came to my mind as clear as any photograph. It was a few miles back. I knew without any question that was where I had to go. I drove straight to the spot and began an exhaustive search along the side of the road on which I had travelled. Nothing! I knew within me that they where there somewhere, but where? Finally in deep discouragement I ignored the mental picture I had received and simply retraced my route from the point of the sale to the point at which I discovered the keys and lock where missing. I retraced this route three times slowly, methodically, and very carefully. Praying constantly for the help I needed. Still nothing! Once again I returned to the intersection that I had seen so clearly in my mind. I couldn't understand why I couldn't find them. Praying again I suddenly knew that they were across the street. How they could have gotten on that side of the street I couldn't even guess. Never the less I knew for sure that they were there.

I should perhaps describe the ice cream vendors outfit that I had on. It consisted of a white smock tied around the waist. A hat that was like one worn by a military officer with the much envied 50 mission crush. Also, of course, the coin changer on a belt around my waist. I must have been a peculiar sight as I trudged up and down the shoulder of the road. I was becoming very self conscious. Still the lock and keys were nowhere to be found.

It occurred to me that I was being made to pour my heart out in prayer. The harder I prayed, the closer I came to the desired answer. I was being humbled and I then realized it. At that moment I knew I had to get down on my knees, right there in front of the passing cars, or the prayer would not be answered. My mind recoiled from the idea. I had always had too much pride.

I had to find the lock and keys, no matter what it cost my dignity. So I did it! I got down on my knees, hat in hand, cars going by, and committed to once more ask in all sincerity for the help I so badly needed. I stared at the empty bare ground between my knees, closed my eyes and began a most sincere and earnest prayer. I poured my heart out as never before. I knew that was what the Lord wanted me to do. When I opened my eyes, there between my knees on the bare ground lay the lock in the exact same spot that only moments before was absolutely empty. There were no keys, just the lock. Oh the joy! Oh the frustration! In that moment I was totally convinced that prayers could be heard and answered, but where were the keys? It seemed certain that they must be here in this area somewhere. I searched, and searched, again and again with great diligence and found nothing. How could this be? This was plain wide open bare ground. There was no place for them to be hidden. I just couldn't understand it. I had no recourse but to ask for help from on high again.

Why Lord? Why are you making me do this? All these people driving by must be wondering if I've lost my mind. I swallowed my pride in an awful gulp, got down and plugged my knees into the same indentations in the dirt. The traffic was going by, the sun was shinning, and I poured my heart out in prayer. When I opened my eyes to stare between my knees at the same spot where the lock had been and was once again empty bare ground, there lay the keys. That day I witnessed with these eyes the movement of solid matter from somewhere unknown to a spot right in front of me that only a moment before had again been bare ground and I learned the value of prayer and the meaning of humility. I can say I value the trait of humility in people more than any other quality.

I was a young man with a serious problem. I desperately needed help. I knew that only the Lord could help me at that moment. When he solved my problem I was very grateful, but I completely missed the real significance of the experience. It wasn't until years later that what had happened really impacted me. Not only had the Lord solved my problem, more importantly He had revealed to me His factual existance as clearly as if He had stood before me and said, "Here I am, know that I exist." I want you to know that I do know, I truly know, and I cherish that knowledge as my most prized possession. I bare you this testimony in the name of Jesus Christ, Amen.

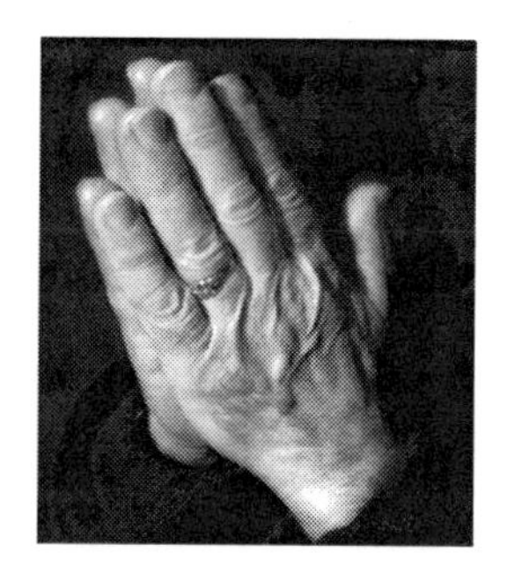

Lily's sweet grass

(fictional story with some history)

Carmody groaned as the roan beneath him stumbled slightly as they crested the rise before them. This old strawberry pony was worth every penny of the ten dollars he had paid for him as many years before. At one dollar a year Gus had saved a fortune in shoe leather. The two of them were well known to those who lived out here on the frontier. Gus had also saved their skins more than once by not only his speed but also his willingness to go where most horses wouldn't consider setting foot.

It was the summer of 1857. Carmody and Gus had taken many a traveler from Omaha to that desolate desert valley on the western slopes of the Wasatch Range of the Rockies. Out there where great towering peaks peered down on the parched landscape, Brother Brigham had declared, "This is the place." Carmody just didn't understand why these "Mormons" were willing to walk all that way, many of them dying in the process. These were a strange people, as they claimed to be. "No, that's peculiar, oh well, it's all the same to me," he mumbled to himself. Anyway he would soon be there in Omaha to pick up the next group.

In the distance he could see where the Platte and the Missouri rivers met. It wouldn't be long now and he and

Gus would have a good meal and some well earned rest. Jonathon Hancock would be pleased to see him a day or two ahead of schedule. Jonathon had a small ranch just outside of town that served as a staging area for "Mormon pioneers" who had arrived from Iowa City, to strike out for the Rockies and the "Land of Deseret" as it was called.

Carmody marveled at the fact that not only did they walk all the way, but because of the high cost of wagons and horses they pushed and pulled handcarts. Let's face it, you could put a lot of handcarts on the trail for a fraction of the cost of just one Conestoga. Most of these folks had lost nearly all of their belongings to looters, having been driven from their homes by mobs or social or economic pressures. Many left just to avoid the horrors that others had faced. Some would never see "the lovely Deseret", he knew so well. Some of these people were foolish, some were courageous, and some were simply followers because that was what they did best. Whatever their reasons were, he had to admit they weren't short on grit. They all had heard the stories of Indian attacks, disease, sudden blinding snow storms that came out of nowhere, accidents, landslides, snakebites, and a long list of other possible disasters. Yet still they came.

He thought of the fields of grain planted along the way to be harvested by those who followed later. He also had to ponder the many "other plantings" along the way that marked the places where so many arrived at the end of their journey prematurely. So many of the children had gone on ahead, by-passing Deseret, but leaping ahead in their long term journey. Young and old, men and women, children and even animals left by the wayside, called to a different path.

He remembered one such incident vividly. The Stanton's were a wonderful family, full of hope and love for each other. Cleon was a big strong man and gentle as they came, Millicent was a diligent and a hard working mother who everyone looked to for her sweet smile and most cheerful attitude. Jacob was a fine young man of ten who was his father's constant shadow. Mary Beth was four months old and very frail. When the baby took sick none were surprised she went so quickly. Cleon dug the grave in the rain and by the next morning was down flat on his back with blood at the corners of his mouth. He had dug so hard and fast trying to be able to get the infant in the ground before the grave was a lake of mud that the heart problem he had kept so quietly hidden announced itself in the worst possible way. Now another grave was needed, a large one. Cheater, the family dog, had refused to leave the grave and had to be put in the handcart that now had to be pushed by Jacob and his mother. Not long after leaving the gravesites the handcart train had to cross the Platte on rafts. Shortly thereafter Cheater ran off in the direction of the river. That night Jacob snuck out of camp. Two days later a third grave was dug by the other two. This one was for Jacob who had tried to rescue Cheater from the muddy waters of the Platte. The dog was found waiting on Cleon's grave. Millicent left Cleon, Jacob, and Mary Beth there with Cheater standing guard for he could not be persuaded to leave. Thereafter it was very rare to see Millicent smile cheerfully, and then only when she spoke of getting to the Celestial Kingdom.

Carmody's mind drifted back over his experiences as Gus clopped along. He had the habit of speaking out loud the thoughts that ran through his mind and any one within earshot would have sworn he was talking to a companion named Gus, and of course he was. He also answered for him. What is it that keeps them coming, some from across the Atlantic? What do they have that made them choose not to renounce their faith and just stay put? How can they work a field in the middle of a wilderness so dedicatedly only to walk away and leave their efforts to be claimed months later by someone they may never know? Soon there will be enough graves to mark the "Mormon Trail" well enough that I'll be out of a job! They sing when things are going well and they sing when things are terrible. They come to each others aid. Most of all they just keep going. Some of them are so good to each other and a few are so upset by the very harsh conditions or tragedies along the way that they want to go back. Who can blame them?

It is amazing the number of strange and miraculous events that seem to be part of their history and everyday life. There seems to be no end of personal tragedy and no running out of mysterious resolutions. He remembered the story he had heard about their crops being attacked by crickets there in Deseret, as they called it. It was said that the hills turned black with them. It seemed nothing could stop them. Had the crops been destroyed many if not all would have starved to death. Then the seagulls seemed to come from nowhere to devour them. It was fortunate that the seagulls could fly and the crickets couldn't. He had personally witnessed injuries and illnesses administered to by "priesthood" holders. Not all survived these calamities, but many did. He knew, 'cause he was there.

There in the distance ahead lay Omaha. It was a raucous and bustling little town. Omaha was also an important staging area for vast numbers of people heading west on the opposite side of the Platte on the Oregon Trail. In a few years it would become known as the Overland Route, the route made famous by the Overland Stage Coach Lines, and the Pony Express and later to become known as the Central Route.

Carmody would have laughed if someone had referred to him as a pioneer. After all, the pioneers were from a long time ago and this was 1857. Wouldn't it be strange to show some of those folks the incredible advances of our modern society? He was deep in thought as Gus plodded along. Imagine what they would have thought of the telegraph. Could they ever have guessed it would be possible to send a message from Washington to Boston in an instant and over a wire? That was 13 years ago and now since those little telegraph companies consolidated last year and became Western Union Telegraph, why now you can send messages all over the country. Wouldn't the pioneers be amazed? Out loud he said, "What else do we have here and now that would surprise them? Come on Gus help me!" "Well, what about the "Iron Horse?" He spoke in the deep voice he always used when speaking for Gus. "Wouldn't that scare the bejeebers out of 'em?" Five years had passed since the first "Iron Horse" rolled into Chicago. "What a sight that must have been. They say it was going almost 50 miles per hour at times. Think of it! How about this, Gus? It's near 10 years already since Sam Colt made the first "Six Shooter." Gus we are living in wondrous times here, times when nearly everything that could be invented has already been invented. I guess that means you and I have about seen it all Gus. Think of it, one day soon these settlers will take the train to Deseret and Oregon and get there in three or four days instead of three or four months. Folks on the other end will know they're comin' at the same time they're leavin'. If there are bandits or Indians to contend with they can send six of them off to the happy hunting ground as fast as they can pull the trigger. No sir Gus, I don't think there is much left for mankind to invent. It's the end of an era, and we lived to see it!"

It was time to take a breather and water Gus and visit Lily. The saddle went thud against the ground. It was cool here under the trees by the edge of the pond. Lily would be right up the hill waiting for him. Gus had his fill of water and was sampling the deep grass along the shore. Carmody thought to himself, "It sure hurts to come here," but he was always glad he did. At the top of the hill the white wooden marker showed the way to where Lily rested. Lily had died in the out break of Variola that took so many four years before. Some people called it smallpox. She was pregnant at the time, doubling his loss. Mrs. Hancock had said she wanted to tell Carmody that there was a way that he and Lily could be together. She said, "I'll explain it to you on your next time through." "I guess it wouldn't hurt to listen," he thought to himself as he sat down by the gravesite.

"Well Sweet, here I am again," he told her. "I've seen a lot and heard a lot from these people I'm taking to the Great Salt Lake, across the Rockies. They have some very strange ideas about things, but somehow I think you'd listen, so I will. They put a lot of stock in God, and if there is one, I know you're with Him. The last trip out was a long one, there were so many delays along the way. We saw some Indians in the distance but they caused us no problems. Not this time. Most of our delays were due to illnesses or accidents. We buried fourteen people along the way on this trip. Twice we had to wait for the river to go down, to get across. Once we waited six days. Gus is fine but he still makes me do all the talking. I sometimes think I'll go gold prospecting when the guide business slows down. I just heard about a big gold strike in Canada, up on the Fraser River. They say it's bigger than California's. The truth is, Sweet, since you're gone I have a hard time stayin' in one place. Oh God, how I miss you. Carmody sat very quiet for a long time, and then shaking himself free from his reverie, he stood up, stretched a mighty stretch and gave Gus a whistle.

Gus dawdled over to him, it was clear the horse was content to stay right there. The water was good, the grass was sweet, but the memories cut deep and wouldn't permit them to stay any longer. Then Carmody saddled up Gus and took him to the edge of the pond for one last drink before this final few miles of trail. As he swung into the saddle, he couldn't help steal a glance at the top of the hill and tipping his hat to Lily, he softly he said, "Be seein' ya, Sweet." Then with a nudge of his heels they loped off toward the Hancock Ranch.

Omaha lay off to his left. It was named after the Omaha Indians, a tribe of the Siouan linguistic stock. The Omaha's are closely related to the Ponca's, Kansas, Osage's, and Quapaw's. He wished all the Indian tribes were as easy goin' as the Omaha's. Even when Lewis and Clark had found them back in 04 they had been very friendly to the whites. They had remained so friendly that they were allowed to select their own reservation site just last year. This old trading post was growing into a real boom town. There was already talk of the railroad coming in within the next three years. It had served as winter quarters late in 46 for the Mormons who had lost 600 people to disease, cold, and starvation that first winter. Chosen as the territorial capital two years ago Omaha was currently being incorporated.

He was received warmly as he lighted off Gus. There were hugs and back slaps and lots of smiles. They sat on the porch that evening after supper and swapped stories and events. Deputy Clyde Hancock, the ranchers brother, had been killed in the line of duty by a chicken thief a few months ago. That a man should die over the theft of a chicken was a sad commentary on how lowly and ruthless society had become in 1857. No wonder the Mormons were leaving. Imagine the irony of leaving your country and nearly all you possessed to escape terrible persecution and injustice, moving to Mexican territory to the middle of a desert wilderness that no one would want in 1847, only to find that with the end of the Mexican War in 1848, that they were once more under the United States flag. They had been leaving for ten years. At first it was to get out of the country and the merciless persecution. Then it was to get out of society. Now it seemed they just sought peace and togetherness. It seemed that each person had their own reasons for being there. There would be a large group and many had already arrived, fearing the numbers would reach the cut off point before they could get there.

Two mornings later the Trail master had called them together to hear the offering of a dedicatory prayer. Now the column stretched out for over half a mile. Carmody had promised Sister Hancock that he would talk to President Young when he arrived in Great Salt Lake City. It would be called that until 1868 when the word "Great" would be dropped from its title. The things that Sister Hancock had explained to him about what his relationship with Lily could be in the future had sparked his interest. He was eager to stop by and visit her on the way.

The tension of quiet anticipation hovered over all. Then the mornings quiet was broken by the bellow of the Trail master. "Let's roll 'em people." Gus stiffened as Carmody swung into the saddle. "Awe Gus, all you want is some more of Lily's sweet grass."

Gene Nay

If I give you the courage
to look inside
will you be brave enough
to open your eyes?

may I cry

(a true story)

My brothers and sisters I'm honored to speak to you today on the subject of repentance. However, I have chosen to discuss the subject in a different manner than you might expect. It pains me to tell you how much my testimony has been weakened and diminished by inappropriate behavior and "sins not repented of" that I have personally witnessed even among us here in attendance. What I have to say may bring some of you a feeling of discomfort. Never the less I feel compelled to bring the problem to your attention, in the hope that badly needed repentance may be applied. I plead with you. Hear my plea. Turn away from sin and temptation.

Here is why I am concerned. I have seen among us the following:

1. **Avoidance** of those people and situations where one may be called on to do something for the Lord. Can't the load be happily shared? Couldn't home and visiting teaching be done for and by all? Must we commit sins of omission?
2. **And**, we say, "We believe in honoring, obeying and sustaining the laws of the land." Yet I have seen

blatant disrespect for such laws. Of course we all know the Lord never really meant for us to observe laws like speed limits, now did He?

3. **And,** I have also seen, disregard for civic responsibilities. Good God loving people are expected to take an interest in the government and its processes, yet I am ashamed to say, sometimes not registering to vote is included in the sins I am listing here for you.
4. **Yes and,** I have even seen the sacred sanctity of the priesthood tarnished by inappropriate looks and poor behavior. In *Matthew 5:28*, the Savior tells us, *"But I say unto you, that whosoever looketh upon a woman"* . . . . and you know the rest.
5. **And,** how can a person rant and rave when they think they've been short-changed a measly 2 cents at a cash register, and yet their lips become magically sealed when they receive 2 dollars too much?
6. **And,** <u>even in the Lord's</u> own house I have heard words that should have no place on the lips of those professing to be His own people. *Mosiah 4 verse 30* says it all when we read there, *"But this much I can tell you, that if ye do not watch yourselves, and your thoughts, and your words, and your deeds, and observe the commandments of God, and continue*

in the faith of what ye have heard concerning the coming of our Lord, even unto the end of your lives, ye must perish. And now, 0 man, remember and perish not."

Now you might say, "Brother Nay, you're just nit-picking. Some of the "sins not repented of" that you've mentioned are just small stuff. My brothers and sisters if we can't control the smallest and easiest sins to correct, how can we ever hope to overcome and conquer the big ones? As Latter-day Saints, we often take comfort from Paul's quotation in the *10th chapter of first Corinthians* where he tells us, *"God will not suffer us to be tempted more than we are able . . ."* However, if we persist in a regrettable behavior to the point of addiction we have already sacrificed our agency and now we are telling ourselves "I can still quit" no matter how many times we again stumble. At this point the adversary has us lying to ourselves and we are in real trouble. If we even think this may be the case we must get help.

I have always thought of our personal testimonies as our "spiritual muscle." It is the strength we take with us when we leave this life. Nothing we can do on this earth is worth more to us than strengthening our testimony because it is the driving force behind every good choice we make.

Without it we face the agony of serious spiritual mistakes as the following incident illustrates.

The bright Arizona sun shimmered down on the colorful flower gardens. It all seemed so perfect a setting for lending comfort to the soul. So, what was this fellow's problem? Well dressed, fifty-ish, just another tourist visiting the Mesa, Temple. His behavior said no! The man pacing back and forth in front of the visitor center seemed unaware of the beautiful buildings, gardens and grounds. It was such a peaceful setting. His uneasiness seemed entirely out of place. Nervously his eyes searched every face as it approached, only to fall disappointedly. It was obvious to anyone who watched that it was most urgent for him to find whomever it was he was searching for.

Occasionally he would move to another area of the grounds and systematically search back and forth among the visitors. Once he had even gone into the visitor center and peered intently through the crowd, but to no apparent avail. Several times a temple guide had started to move toward him to offer assistance only to find himself being warned off by the man's demeanor. Not that this stranger was intimidating, rather he was just busy in his quest and seemed to prefer to be left alone.

This had gone on for quite some time. The man noticed that three of the guides seemed to be discussing him. Probably trying to determine which of them could best cut through his invisible barrier and see if this stranger would accept some assistance. However with the sifting of those coming, through those going, the guides found other priorities among the curious visitors. It was just as well though, for the man had once more struck out on his lonely vigil. Again he covered every square inch of the grounds, searching every face he found. After some time he again appeared in the visitor center. The guides again began talking among themselves and apparently had elected a tall elderly gentleman to approach this stranger. "Is there some way I can help you sir?" The guide had gently spoken as he came close to the man. "No thank you," was the reply as the stranger deftly moved away, only to be once again caught up in his search.

It soon became obvious that the strangers' determination was loosing its battle to despair. He looked exhausted, crestfallen, and dejected. His shoulders slumped in disappointment. The search seemed to have ended as strangely and quietly as it had begun. With downcast eyes he approached the guides, passed them by, and then suddenly stopped. He seemed to realize the image he had been creating. With effort he straightened, turned and walked right up to them. "Gentlemen I know I must look a little peculiar considering my behavior here these last few hours and I feel an explanation is in order. You see I'm looking for a young man that I am concerned about. He seems firmly dedicated to the teachings of the gospel. However I sense a certain weakness in him. Yet he has so many blessings. He'd be in his early twenties with a lovely bride and an infant son. They are coming here to be sealed. I'm afraid I've missed him and I needed so much to speak to him. I wished to tell him how important it is that he keeps the vows he is about to take. I so wanted to warn him that he could lose so much if he isn't careful, and to hold on tightly to the principles he so strongly believes in."

"Perhaps he's just late," said the taller guide. "Yes," added the short heavyset fellow, offering hope. "No", said the stranger shifting dejectedly, "It seems I'm looking for miracles rather then dealing with answers." "What do you mean," asked the tall man? The stranger began to tremble, "It was so important to find him but I'm too late you see, thirty years too late gentlemen, the young man I hoped to find was myself." The stranger sadly walked away. This story is true, it happened in the spring of 1983.

What terrible price did this man pay for his lack of repentance? How desperate must he have been to ask the

Lord to let him be carried back in time so that he could warn himself of what was going to happen? The words of a poet express exactly what "sins not repented of" can be. This poem is titled;

I'm not the man . . .

I'm not the man I could have been
and I may never be,
because I've witnessed so much sin
and it's affected me.

I will tell you of these sins,
some I still can see.
I fear that they've forever changed
the me I'd hoped to be.

I saw a man that said,
"Follow my example."
He took advantage of his friends
and that was just a sample.

Then there's the man who lives
as though he's clean and pure,
who takes back all he gives
plus double to be sure.

I’ve seen a man who broke his word
and turned his face away.
He rejected all he heard
no matter what they’d say.

I’ve seen an awful pride
keep one from doing right.
Not man enough to look inside
he kept it up for spite.

One brought pain and heartbreak
caused by negligence,
and then he tried to cover up
by pleading innocence.

You may say it’s not enough
these reasons that I give.
You say it’s up to me to choose
the way I want to live.

There are more sins I have seen
worse than all before.
Some of them have been so bad
let me tell you more.

I have even seen a man
so woe-be-gone and lazy,
were someone to depend on him
he nearly drove them crazy.

There's a man that played with minds
and led them far astray.
He convinced them they could wrong
and never have to pay.

And then a man who's wife
was good and pure and chaste.
He chose to live a sinful life
and made it all a waste.

I've seen a servant of the Lord
raise his arm in hate,
then tell others "Drop the sword
and find the Pearly Gate."

A man I know shunned his God
to go another way,
in spite of all his friends and family
tried in vain to say.

I've seen so many ugly things
  it really is a shame.
This is why I have to tell you
  where to lay the blame.

If you wonder why I blame
  all the sins I've shown,
I'm not the man I could have been
  these sins are all my own.

Gene Nay

My brothers and sisters I am the poet who wrote this. I am also the stranger who searched the crowds at the Mesa Temple looking for myself. Every sin I've listed in my talk and my poem is my own and there are so many more. Long ago I turned my back and walked away from the Lord. At times I even ran, putting as much distance between us as possible, for years and years leaving the Lord far behind. When I at last turned around to experience the great distance I had placed between us, there He was as always, with his open arms beckoning me to the safety of his Celestial embrace. Now, because I'm not the man I could have been, I plead to my dear Lord with all my heart,

Oh Lord please,
Capture my wild soul.
Tame my rebellious heart.
Curb my wish to flee.
Anchor my curious mind.
Hobble my wandering feet.
Break my determination to resist thee.
Win my desire to serve thee.
Hedge up my route of escape from thee.
All this I ask, that I may never leave thee.

I thank thee Lord that thou hast,
let me turn from the light,
just long enough to fear the dark,
And let me taste of enough evil,
that I may be reviled by it,
And suffered me to fall,
less times than
I have been able to rise.
Now, oh Lord, strengthen me
to desire sin no more.

Brothers and Sisters, it is by "sins ***not*** repented of" that our testimony of God's existence is diminished! It is by "sins repented of" that our testimony is magnified! It is also by our self-righteousness that we lock ourselves out of exaltation. And, it is by our humility that we open the gates to Glory.

My hero of the holy scriptures is not a prophet, not a warrior, neither a king nor an angel. My hero of the scriptures is found in *Luke 18 verses 9 thru 14. "And he spake this parable unto certain which trusted in themselves that they were righteous, and despised others: Two men went up into the temple to pray; the one a Pharisee, and the other a publican. The Pharisee stood and prayed thus with himself, "God I thank thee, that I am not as other men are, extortioners, unjust, adulterers, or even as this publican. I fast twice in the week, I give tithes of all that I possess." And the publican, standing afar off, would not lift up so much as his eyes unto heaven, but smote upon his breast, saying, God be merciful unto me a sinner. I tell you this man went down to his house justified rather than the other: for everyone that exalteth himself shall be abased; and he that humbleth himself shall be exalted."* The Pharisee in his pride judged others as lower than himself. The publican in his humility judged himself as lowest of all.

It is because the Lord has been so close to me when I thought myself so far from Him that I still have hope. I know of God's kingdom and that my Savior lives, and now you know why my testimony is weaker than it could be. Even so, we must remember that we all fall short of perfection. In *1st John 1:8* we read, *"If we say that we have no sin, we deceive our selves and the truth is not in us."* May we never forget that the Savior came to redeem and take home the sinners, like me and all of you who are not perfect, that we may become so.

I love you my brothers and sisters and I implore you to please, please repent. I leave my "gentle thoughts" with you in the only name given by which anyone can return to our Heavenly Father, the sacred name of His son Jesus Christ. Amen.

Gene Nay

Oh poet!
Speak the words
of your heart.

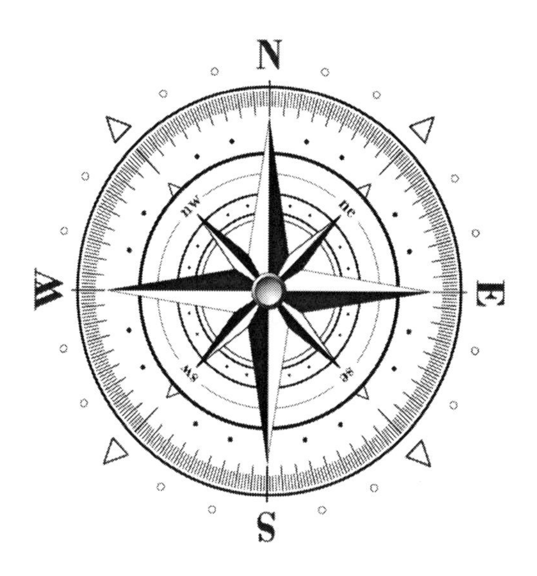

Section 4 Guest Poets . . .

Guest Poets

Would you like to see your own words in print? Would you like them to be viewed world wide? We are working to make it happen. Be sure to visit our website at www. holdagentlethought.com presently under construct-ion and click on **Guest Poets**, soon to be up. The following pages include two examples:

Author: James Wayne Howell

When Jimbo, as we called him, was just under 2 years of age his mother and I had just placed him in the back seat of the car. He was sitting in the middle of her spread out fur coat, a favorite thing for him to do. We placed the groceries we had just purchased beside him and had become involved in a brief discussion. Upon finishing our rather lengthy brief discussion we got into the car and marveled at how quiet the child was. Curiosity got the best of us and we simultaneously turned to the back seat and discovered that "chef Jimbo" was busy scrambling up a huge omelet of about a dozen eggs, shells and all, in the middle of moms fur coat. I mention this to illustrate how young he was when he began to show his creative aptitude. After many years this came from my adult Jim.

the Day of the Giants by James Wayne Howell

God has breathed life and love into my spirit.
forgive my selfish ways
and the contempt I feel for the majority,
yet the humor is so overwhelming
that I forgot to laugh.

I was born into my own universe.
It was as the garden of God
and I was pleased,
and being so young,
I had the right
To be a young King,
and I was much pleased.

There was a Giant in my house.
He was a bit verbose
and lumbered around my house
doing those things that Giants do.
I am a very young King
of about 1-2-3-4-5, I forget,
things of this nature
did not concern me.

The Giant was a good Giant. I think.
A perfectionist to be sure,
as the Giant found more pleasure
in my cartoons than I,
so I thought I would like to be
a Giant like him.

I was very big for my size,
but my body wasn't,
but that didn't stop me.
I could lift the heaviest boxes.
I could lift the whole house if he would let me,
because I am a Giant.

The Giant could scare away the monsters
under my bed.
He could laugh
At the monsters in my closet
and they would go away
and he made me believe
in a jolly old fat man.

I had the best Giant,
better than anyone in all the universe.
Children live forever because
God loves us more,
but Giants such as mine

have to go where Giants go,
but I was not old enough
to go where my Giant was going,
so I had to learn to be a Giant
by myself,
with God's help to be sure.

I love my Giant
and wherever He is,
what ever Giant stuff my Giant is doing now
I want Him to know
that if my Giant is sick or hurt
I will take care of Him,
Just step on the ground
very loudly
and I will come.

I also wanted to say, "I love you".
So as the Giant looks at the sun
He is granted one wish,

even though Giants don't need to wish
for they are great warriors in life,
Captains, Kings,
Friend to the truth.
Thank you.

I will never have a Giant
or ever want another Giant.
Feelings of a great and humble Giant.

Just wanted to say,
May your road be tough enough
to give you strength
and your rainbows a gift from God.
—The Day of the Giants-
Your son
Jim Howell

PS:
I have many wishes ,
one is that your heart is strong,
your truth is without flaw,
and that you yell and challenge life
with every step.
Never give in,
or they'll steal your smile.

You're always welcome
at my campfire,
Thank you sir,
Thank you Dad
Thank you, my only Giant.
God bless.

Author: Tish Roberts

This poet gave me one of the most interesting afternoons I have ever experienced. She is a most gifted lady who knows more about almost everything than one can imagine. The only reason I say almost everything is because I didn't ask her about absolutely everything. She's a gifted teacher and should have been a major athlete with stamina beyond measure. If you haven't yet read Mothers Day in Section 3, I think you will enjoy getting acquainted with Tish.

WHAT CHANGED THE CHILD? by Tish Roberts

What changed the child;
Who ran so free and wild?
The one who laughed so free
And danced and skipped with glee?
What changed the ready smile;
of the child sweet and mild?

What changed this little one;
And took away the sense of fun?
What caused the fear and lack of trust?
Now blown away like grains of dust.
What put the look of fear and alarm;
Into the eyes that once were warm?

Could it be the child just grew old;
And the sunshine all turned cold?
Or did someone do a terrible harm;
That killed the spirit once so warm?
Was this done as a lesson to be taught;
To change the child, and all for naught?

Please take away this added weight,
A child can't live with all this hate.

Thank you for reading this book. I hope you were able to find some things within these pages that reminded you of some of your own experiences. It is my most sincere desire that you find enough comfort from these contents that you will re-read them and re-experience your own special moments, and please always . . .

. . . hold a gentle thought.

Gene Nay

See my message to
you at the rear of this book.

Here's a special message for you.

As the author, I want this book to present itself to you with dignity rather than to have it be used as a soapbox opportunity for the famous. My hope is for it to live in your home as a "good book" and not as a "brief interruption for a commercial announcement." You won't find any illustrious dignitaries, name dropping referrals or money making endor$ement$ pasted to its cover. The only endorsement I'm looking for is one that comes from you. If you should find pleasure, comfort, enjoyment, or disappointment between the covers of this book, *please,* let me know. You will also find no ads on my web site unless placed there without my consent. I want the future of the book and the website, if there is a future for them, to stand on the value of what they say to you and not who says it for them. If these words are accepted by the public, I have more to add. Book two waits in the wings. I also am waiting, to hear from you.

Gene Nay

www.holdagentlethought.com

CPSIA information can be obtained at www.ICGtesting.com
Printed in the USA
BVOW07s1655200415

396891BV00001BA/5/P